ENDORSEMENTS

"Asia's *The Curious Kid's Science Book* is not just another book of experiments to fill a rainy day. This book guides parents through the process of inspiring a sense of curiosity in children, and developing a set of skills to help them problem solve, and be scientific thinkers. Through real-life experience, Citro demonstrates that even very young children can design experiments, document progress, and share their discoveries in a meaningful way. While the book is full of easy, fun, and meaningful science activities, its real value is its approach to helping parents inspire a sense of exploration and discovery that will benefit their children long after they have grown."

—Bob Pflugfelder, Founder of ScienceBob.com,
seen on *Jimmy Kimmel Live* and *Live with Kelly and Michael*,
author of the *Nick and Tesla* series

"This is a delightful book that draws on a child's natural curiosity to impart the basics of scientific inquiry—from question to hypothesis to experiment to the results and conclusions. Children will love it and parents will learn some things, too."

—Dr. Henry L. Roediger III,
James S. McDonnell Distinguished University Professor,
Washington University in St. Louis,
author of *Make It Stick: The Science of Successful Learning*

"Asia Citro is a welcome new voice in the world of science education. As an educator and mother of two young children, she has a deep understanding that children are naturally curious, ask good questions, and freely investigate the world around them when given the chance. What *The Curious Kid's Science Book* does so well, which so many science books for kids tend to miss, is the celebration of this innate curiosity and penchant for experimentation. With this understanding in hand, this book encourages children not to replicate tried and true science projects, but to ask their own questions and think like real scientists! From building a hypothesis to testing out theories, *The Curious Kid's Science Book* will harness the scientist inside children and their adult counterparts. Bravo!"

—Rachelle Doorley, Arts Educator at TinkerLab.com,
author of *Tinkerlab: A Hands-On Guide for Little Inventors*

"I am a firm believer in the power of children's questions to open doors to discovery. Asia Citro has unlocked that power in this collection of explorations that even the youngest of scientists will enjoy."

—Tom Robinson, National Board Certified Teacher,
bestselling author of *The Everything Kids' Science Experiments Book*

"Perhaps children are the best scientists and explorers because they aren't afraid to ask the question 'Why?' I encourage you to use the easy-to-do hands-on activities in this book to fuel your children's innate creativity and problem-solving skills. Plus, without knowing it, they'll have fun learning science and math!"

—Captain Wendy Lawrence, Former NASA astronaut

"Based on the premise that young children are curious, observant, and determined problem solvers, *The Curious Kid's Science Book* is a brilliant resource that will get teachers and parents of young children excited about exploring the world of science in the classroom or at home. Asia has photographed a wonderful and broad collection of easy-to-put-into-action scientific investigations and shared them along with simple tips for keeping science fun and engaging. As you and your child get busy exploring the ideas shared throughout Asia's book, your young scientist will be developing the confidence and basic skills needed to be a capable and competent problem solver in many areas of life!"

—Deborah J. Stewart, Founder of TeachPreschool.org,
author of *Ready for Kindergarten!*

"As an educator who values creativity, discovery, exploring, and experimenting, I'm thrilled to recommend Asia Citro's science activity book that encourages kids to ask their own questions. Kids will explore answers and investigate their own outcomes, building on curiosity and creative inspiration. I especially like that easy-to-find materials are used. What a playful, powerful jump into science!"

—MaryAnn F. Kohl,
bestselling author of over 20 children's art books

The Curious Kid's Science Book

100+ Creative Hands-on Activities for Ages 4–8

Asia Citro, MEd

author of *150+ Screen-Free Activities for Kids*

THE
INNOVATION
PRESS

Published by
The Innovation Press
P.O. Box 2584, Woodinville, WA 98072-2584. U.S.A.
www.theinnovationpress.com

Citro, Asia.
The curious kid's science book : 100+ creative hands-on
activities for ages 4-8 / Asia Citro, M. Ed.
     pages cm
     Includes index.
     LCCN 2015903881
     ISBN 978-1-943147-00-7
     ISBN 978-1-943147-01-4
     ISBN 978-1-943147-02-1
     ISBN 978-1-943147-03-8

     1. Science--Experiments. 2. Science--Study and
teaching (Primary)--Activity programs. 3. Science
projects. I. Title.

     Q164.C455 2015   507.8
                    QBI15-600075

Printed and bound in China.
Production Date: 05/2015
Batch Number: 53799-0
Plant Location: Printed by Everbest Printing Co. Ltd., Nansha, China

10 9 8 7 6 5 4 3 2 1

Photography by Asia Citro.
Lunchbox font by Kimmy Design.
Frente font by Frente.
Cover design by Kerry Ellis.

To Bubba and Goose, always.

Acknowledgments

Thank you to my family for all of your support. I couldn't have written and photographed this book without the help and cooperation of my kids and the child care provided by my husband, mom, and mother-in-law.

A big thank-you to Nicole Nuckley, Melissa Jenkins, Henry Valz, Jenny Shibayama, Anita MacPherson, and Nicole Flynn for double-checking my scientific accuracy. And thank you to my mom, my husband, Jessica Petersen, Rachael Brown, Stephanie Haass, and Kerissa Potter for all of your help writing and refining the introduction and the summary of the book. Thank you to my talented and patient graphic designer, Kerry Ellis, for bringing my vision for the book to life. And thank you to my editor, Cynthia Reeh, for helping me with all the finishing touches.

Thank you to MaryAnn Kohl for everything! You continue to be an inspiration and a huge resource, not to mention a great friend.

Thank you to all of our *Fun at Home with Kids* blog readers and all of our *150+ Screen-Free Activities for Kids* book readers for your wonderful comments, messages, and photos. We love hearing from you and your support means the world to us!

Thank you to Discount School Supply and Shady Oak Butterfly Farm for providing some of the materials in this book. And thank you to Tiffany Ard of Nerdy Baby for allowing us to use one of your amazing prints in the book.

Thank you to Chelsey Marashian (of BuggyandBuddy.com), Jessica Petersen (of Play-Trains.com), Suja Balaji (of KidsPlayBox.com), Jenny Shibayama, and Helen Buttemer for inspiring an activity in the book with your work. And thank you to Stephanie Haass for taking and providing the two photos of your goggle-wearing scientists.

Thank you to my friends for all of your support. Your insight into what would be useful in a science book helped shape this book. And an extra thank-you to those of you who let me set up a miniature science lab inside your home with your children.

And finally, thank you to my wonderful, creative, silly, and brilliant young scientist friends. Your enthusiasm was such a big help to me as I was writing these experiments. Thank you for being awesome.

Table of Contents

⚡ = activities that don't require preparation ahead of time

⚡ = activities that don't require preparation ahead of time

CHAPTER 4: Engineering 109

⚡ = activities that don't require preparation ahead of time

⚡ = activities that don't require preparation ahead of time

= activities that don't require preparation ahead of time

⚡ = activities that don't require preparation ahead of time

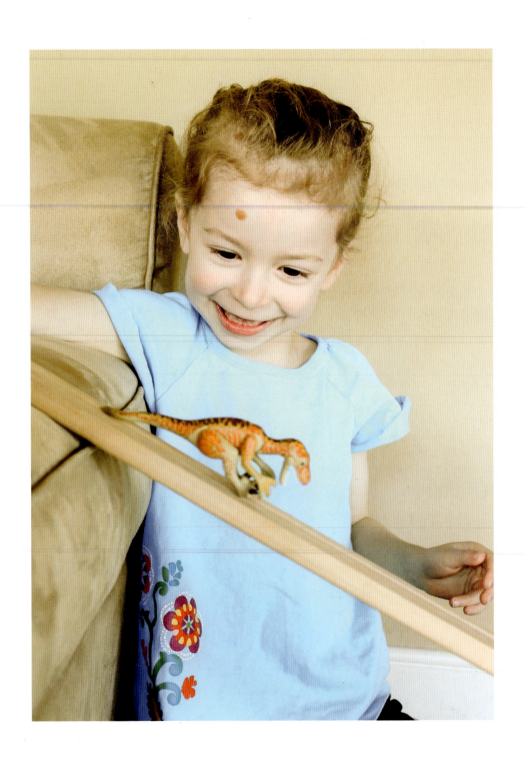

Introduction

My 5-year-old daughter is playing in our living room, using a piece of wood as a ramp for two Matchbox cars. This piece of wood has a nice groove in the middle, making it a perfect little ramp. "Mom!" she exclaims. "Look! One of the cars falls off the ramp every time, but the other car stays on the whole way down." She sits for a moment, pondering the ramp and the two cars. Then she smiles and flips the cars over. "I get it! This one has bigger wheels, so they don't fit all the way in the middle of the ramp and that makes it fall."

> **We can best help children learn... by paying attention to what they do: answering their questions...and helping them explore the things they are most interested in.**
> –JOHN HOLT

"Ooh, interesting theory," I say. "Could you find a way to test that with more cars?" She nods and hops off to dig through her toys, triumphantly returning with a monster truck sporting wide wheels and a Mustang with narrower wheels. She sends the cars down the ramp, followed quickly by: "I knew it! The monster truck has wheels that are too big. It doesn't fit and it falls off, too!" Shortly thereafter, a plastic velociraptor slides its way completely down the ramp. She excitedly checks and yes, his feet and tail are narrow enough to fit in the groove.

After inspecting the ramp for a minute, my daughter's face lights up as she asks, "Mom! Can we build a seesaw to weigh some of my toys with this ramp?" I nod and watch as her eyes dart around the room looking for the items she'll need. Minutes later she's weighing various toys on a balance she created from a piece of wood trim teetering on a small plastic box.

As a science teacher, I would like to see a change in how we traditionally approach science with our children. Science is not about following someone else's experiment step by step, or just watching exciting demonstrations. It is not about reciting scientific facts or vocabulary.

It's about asking your own questions and making your own investigations—two things young children are very good at! Using simple materials from a grocery store or your house, the activities in this book encourage children to explore science in an open-ended, playful, and powerful way.

Every baby knows the **scientific method!**

1 Make an observation.

2 Form a hypothesis.

3 Perform the experiment.

4 Analyze the data.

5 Report your findings.

6 Invite others to reproduce the results.

Courtesy of Tiffany Ard

CHILDREN ARE BORN SCIENTISTS

Babies and toddlers learn about their world by forming questions and experimenting to find the answers. Have you seen a baby or toddler drop food from a high chair over and over to see what happens? Children are born scientists.

Young children are curious, observant, and determined problem solvers. They are full of questions and excited to learn more. These are not only traits of a successful scientist, but also traits necessary to succeed in STEM-related careers (science, technology, engineering, and mathematics). Giving children the chance to make their own experiments allows these natural skills to grow and bloom.

SCIENCE DOESN'T NEED TO BE COMPLICATED

Young children are interested in the simple materials around them; you don't need to use special materials or complicated experiments to get their attention. Simple materials like seeds, water, and baking soda are engaging and are great for experimenting. This book has over 100 simple, easy, and fun activities that can be done with little to no setup using materials easily found in your home or in a grocery store.

> **"All the world is a laboratory to the inquiring mind."**
> –MARTIN FISCHER

Professional scientists conduct very detailed and tightly controlled experiments. Young children don't need to be held to such rigorous standards. Homes are not equipped with a professional laboratory where you can carefully control every variable. Do your best to encourage accuracy, but remember that a simplified approach is fine. No one expects a 5-year-old's experiment to be as complex or accurate as an adult's.

EXPERIMENTS DON'T NEED TO WORK PERFECTLY TO BE VALUABLE

Sometimes your experiment will fail. Sometimes your experiment will give you more questions than answers. This is the nature of science. Even failed experiments are valuable; children can learn from what went wrong and apply that knowledge to future experiments. Science is rarely cut and dry, and it is rarely perfect. As such, many of the activities are intentionally vague and open-ended. The challenges activities in particular are intended to involve multiple attempts for a child to learn through trial and error.

FOCUS ON DEVELOPING YOUR CHILD'S NATURAL SCIENTIFIC SKILLS

Science education for young children should foster their natural scientific tendencies to observe, question, and experiment. Allowing children to have the time and space to explore in an open-ended way helps them to develop these skills, and giving them opportunities to practice designing simple experiments allows them to take on the role of scientists. In real life, there are several ways to investigate a question. Rather than providing just one way with set measurements and directions, this book gives children the chance to use their problem-solving skills to create their own way to investigate questions. Through challenging them to lead experiments, children will gain experience evaluating their work and learning from their mistakes.

> **"Many adults, including educators, tend to underestimate children's capacity to learn science core ideas and practices in the early years and fail to provide the opportunities and experiences for them to foster science skills (NRC 2007, p. vii)."**
> —NATIONAL SCIENCE TEACHERS ASSOCIATION POSITION STATEMENT ON EARLY CHILDHOOD SCIENCE EDUCATION, 2014

THE SKILLS GAINED FROM THIS BOOK WILL HELP YOUR CHILD SUCCEED

Over the past two decades, U.S. schools have begun to embrace child-led science. Unlike in past generations when the laboratory portion of science was about following the directions of others, today's children will be asked to develop their own questions and experiments. The skills gained from doing the experiments in this book will help your child succeed in school. Additionally, the experience of asking questions and designing experiments will give your child the foundation needed to come up with their own science fair projects.

The activities in this book are designed to foster problem-solving skills that will be useful throughout your child's life, even if your child doesn't ultimately end up in a STEM-related career. The ability to design an experiment to answer a question is relevant to all professions, even if the question is about marketing or management instead of laboratory science.

How to Use This Book

The activities in this book are centered around easy-to-find materials that engage the curiosity of young children. Each chapter begins with the skills or techniques needed for the activities along with a supply list to cover everything needed in that chapter. I also provide age-appropriate explanations to describe some of the concepts your child may uncover as they experiment. Some children will be very interested in the background information, whereas others will not. The book's emphasis is on children discovering this information for themselves, so please don't worry if your child isn't interested in sitting down and listening to the explanations.

> **"We should not teach children the sciences, but give them a taste for them."**
>
> –JEAN JACQUES ROUSSEAU

Following each chapter's introduction, children are invited to (1) explore a material, (2) design an experiment to answer a question about the material, or (3) challenge themselves to create something. I had the help of several young scientists as I wrote, and throughout the book you'll find some examples of how they approached the activity, along with their ages.* The examples are not meant to dictate how your child should run the experiment, but they can serve as guidance if you're not sure where to start. The activities are not presented in a specific order, so feel free to jump around. After completing the activities in a chapter, I hope that your child will continue to explore the topic by asking their own follow-up questions or designing their own experiments (prompts are provided for each experiment under Advanced Level).

* Fictitious names are used for all the children in this book.

Allowing children to follow their interests and develop their curiosity makes such a positive difference in their experience of science. They are excited and engaged learners, proud of their discoveries and their competency as problem-solvers, and eager to ask questions that enable them to better understand their world.

Asking Questions

Not every question your child asks will lend itself to an experiment. The activities in this book are designed to familiarize you and your child with the types of questions that can be answered by an experiment. Each experiment has an intermediate and an advanced level. The intermediate level gives some gentle guidance on how to design your experiment to help ease the transition from the traditional style of science experiment where the question, method, and measurements are all predetermined. At the advanced level, children are prompted to ask their own questions about a phenomenon and design their own experiments.

To help your child develop a question for an experiment, you could ask: "I wonder what would happen if…" or ask if they have a comparison question, for example: "I wonder if <blank> is better/faster/larger than <blank>." After every experiment, you'll see a prompt to ask your child follow-up questions. Included in most experiments is a box detailing how one of my young scientist helpers decided to approach the experiment, along with any of their questions. At the advanced level, this book challenges your child to either come up with their own follow-up question or to develop an experiment to answer my helper's question. The ultimate goal of this book is to give you and your child the confidence to embark on your own explorations.

Asking your child questions at the end of the experiment is a great way to encourage them to analyze and develop their own explanations for what they see. Example questions to ask as children are looking at experimental results are:

- What do you think is happening?
- Why do you think this is happening? (Can they support this by using data they collected during the experiment?)
- What do you still wonder about?

Their explanations may or may not be correct. More importantly, they are strengthening their skills of inferring and using data to form explanations.

Basic Experimental Design

Most homes aren't equipped to carry out experiments that test exactly one variable—that's why scientists work in laboratories where variables can be tightly controlled and monitored. As I'll discuss in the next section, one of the most important things in a successful experiment is changing only one variable at a time. Because you are doing science with small children in a home, daycare, or school setting, it's not possible to eliminate all other variables. As long as you are focusing your child on changing only one thing and you are doing your best to keep everything else the same, it is enough for our purposes. For instance, if you are experimenting with how much water a seed needs to sprout, you would change only the amount of water you are using each time—because the amount of water is what you are testing. You would use the same type of seeds, the same amount and type of soil, same amount of sunlight, etc. By changing only one thing at a time, you can better study the effects of that change. If you change several things, you don't know which change is having which effect.

As children get older, their teachers will begin applying scientific terminology to the following steps. For our purposes, I leave out that terminology and focus on keeping it simple and accessible.

Here are the simplified steps to designing an experiment:

1. Ask a question you can answer with an experiment (see Asking Questions).
   Let's use an example question: "I wonder which my cat will like more—cold or warm drinking water?"

2. Guess what the answer will be.

Sometimes kids balk because they don't know the answer. Remind them that it's OK to be wrong, and you can model guessing yourself. Don't worry if they don't join in with a guess right away. Following our example question, an example guess might be: "I think my cat will like cold water most."

3. Decide on the steps of your experiment.

One of the most vital things to impart to your little scientist when it comes to designing an experiment is changing only one thing at a time. Every time I design an experiment with a young child, I remind them to "change ONE thing and keep everything else the same!" This is necessary for a successful experiment.

Following our example question, the thing we are changing is the temperature of the water. That means we need to do our best to keep everything else the same. In this case, we'd need to use the same cat, the same amount of water (i.e., 4 cups of water), the same size/shape of bowl for the water (i.e., two matching bowls from your kitchen), the same location for the water (i.e., both on the ground side by side), and the same timing (i.e., you wouldn't want to try cold water in the morning and then try warm water in the afternoon). If your child needs help with determining what things will need to stay the same, you can always phrase each variable as a question: "Should we use different water dishes or the same?" The steps in our experiment might include:

1. I will measure 4 cups of warm water into one white bowl from our kitchen and then I will measure 4 cups of cold water into the other white bowl from our kitchen.
2. I will set both bowls next to each other on the ground in the kitchen in the morning.
3. I will put the cat in front of both bowls.
4. I will dab a small amount of water from each on the cat's nose.

4. Decide how to measure your results.

Kids don't have a lot of experience measuring results, so they often need guidance. If possible, try to offer some ideas by asking your child what they will look for. For example, you might ask: Which bowl does the cat drink more from?

Which bowl does the cat go to first? How does the cat react to the water they drink—does it immediately stop drinking after one sip? We don't need to get too technical when recording data with small children. As long as they understand the concept of gathering data, they can use impressions rather than actual measurements to answer their questions. If you have the tools (for example, a ruler, thermometer, and stopwatch), this is a great opportunity to incorporate math and give them additional practice gathering measurements.

5. Answer your question!

Sometimes you won't be able to answer the question and that is OK. That happens to scientists, too. Maybe your answer will be something like: "My cat wouldn't drink, so I don't know which water he likes better." Or maybe: "My cat drank some water from each dish, so I can't tell which water he likes better." Whether your results definitively answer your question ("My cat drank only the cold water. I think he likes cold water best.") or not, be sure to talk about what you learned. In science, even failed experiments are valuable. Rather than feeling defeated that the experiment didn't work, talk about what you learned from the experiment. Maybe it will help you design a different experiment, or maybe it will lead you to a new question to test!

Some final thoughts on experimental design:

- Rather than dictating how to run the experiment, you are asking your child for their input every step of the way. Let the experiment be theirs as much as possible. On the other hand, for the sake of practicality and expense, it is not necessary to let them do everything they wish. For example, your child may want to test 2 cups of soap each time with a baking soda and vinegar experiment. It would be fine to say something like: "That sounds like fun. Unfortunately, soap is expensive, so let's work with a smaller amount. Would you like to use 1, 2, or 3 teaspoons of soap each time?"

- Sometimes children want to test amounts that are very similar each time and may not produce much change. For example, they might want to test watering plants with 40 mL, 45 mL, and 50 mL of water. You could encourage them to choose either a very small or a very large number. Or you could let them run the experiment and then talk about how all of your results were similar because all the amounts of water were very similar. They might like to run a follow-up experiment using bigger differences in the amounts of water to see what happens.

- The important thing to remember is that you are experimenting, and that your experiments may not turn out perfectly. Kids often spill or are inexact with their measurements and this is fine.

Science and Art

Writing down steps and recording data are fundamental practices in science. While experimenting, encourage your child to label their experiments as much as possible. In most of the photos, I intentionally removed the labels to avoid providing suggestions on what to do. However, I do strongly suggest labeling all the parts of your experiment (for example, if you are watering a plant with 45 mL of water every other day, note this using a tape label somewhere on the plant pot) so you don't forget what you've done!

Samantha, age 5

I believe in the value of keeping a scientific notebook, but not if it interrupts a child's focus or becomes a chore. For most children ages 4 to 8 years old, writing in a scientific journal as they go will interrupt their thinking. Instead, I suggest that the adult writes

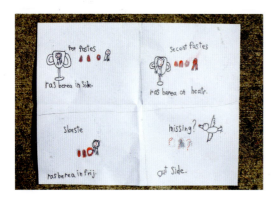

Daisy, age 7

down measurements or any other noteworthy bits of information. After the experiment, inviting your child to draw what they learned is a great way to encourage them to process the experiment. You can offer the measurements you recorded to add to their drawing if they wish. Art is a fantastic way for young children to solidify and summarize their scientific findings.

Science Supplies

Many of the supplies you need for the activities in this book are in your kitchen or pantry. Most of the remaining items can be found at a grocery store or the Dollar Tree. Each activity has a list of suggested supplies (in many activities, children are encouraged to think creatively and use what they have on hand). At the beginning of each chapter is a checklist of everything you need to complete all activities in that chapter.

If you're looking to get started right away, here's a quick list of the most common supplies suggested in the book:

- ☐ Plastic cups (short and tall)
- ☐ Ziplock bags
- ☐ Masking tape
- ☐ Potting soil
- ☐ Food coloring (our favorite is neon)
- ☐ Cotton balls
- ☐ Coffee filters (the big white basket kind)
- ☐ Salt
- ☐ Straws
- ☐ Children's safety goggles

- ☐ Sugar
- ☐ Cooking oil
- ☐ Vinegar
- ☐ Dish soap
- ☐ Corn syrup
- ☐ Cotton swabs
- ☐ Lemon juice
- ☐ Baking soda
- ☐ Pinto beans

The supplies listed above along with this book also make a great creative DIY Science Kit gift for holidays or birthdays!

OPTIONAL SUPPLIES

If you'd like to encourage your child's math skills, consider including a stopwatch, set of plastic beakers, thermometer, pipettes, and tape measure. Don't expect your child to be able to use them accurately at first. These tools generally take a fair bit of practice before children can use them well. If you decide to include them with your science supplies, I recommend introducing the tools on their own before incorporating them into the activities in the book. Start by allowing your child to play with them. If your child needs some prompting to start their explorations, you can offer little challenges, such as:

- Use a stopwatch to time how long it takes to run a lap through the house.
- Use a tape measure to measure how high off the ground your bed is.
- Use a thermometer to measure how warm your bathwater is.
- Use a beaker to measure how much water you usually drink with dinner.

The beaker pictured is part of a plastic set from Amazon; the remaining items pictured are from Discount School Supply and are available through their website.

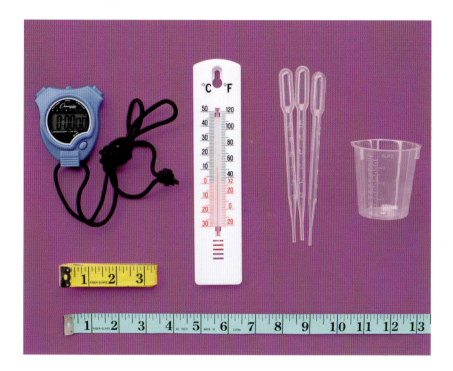

Chapter 1
Plants and Seeds

INTRODUCTION

In this chapter, you'll explore how plants and seeds grow. For the experiments that require plants, you can either grow your own or you can buy inexpensive (or clearance) plants from a garden store or home improvement store. You could even use weeds from your backyard as your experimental plants! Our favorite seeds for sprouting are beans and peas because they are hardy enough to survive frequent exploration by little hands and manage fluctuations in water, heat, and sunlight well. You can also find beans and peas year-round at your grocery store. A variety of dried beans is usually found on the same grocery store aisle as rice, packaged in a bag (pinto beans are my favorite), and dried peas are usually found nearby, also packaged in bags labeled as green or yellow split peas. Depending on the brand, the seeds are sometimes sterilized, which means that though they will grow, they will not flower or grow produce. If observing that stage is a priority for you, I recommend getting your bean and pea seeds from a garden store.

GROWING YOUR OWN PLANTS

Our favorite method of growing plants works year-round. We call it the "sprouting bag" and it functions like a miniature greenhouse. To make a sprouting bag, you need a paper towel or some cotton balls. Get them wet and then squeeze them out. When you place them in the bag they should be damp, but not wet. After you have placed the damp cotton balls or paper towel in your bag, add a few seeds and seal the bag. Keep it someplace warm, or tape it up in your window to watch the seeds sprout and grow. Shortly after sprouting, the growing plant will need to be planted in a cup with soil. Any container can be a plant pot, even old (cleaned) milk containers with the tops cut off. Just be sure that whichever container you use has a few holes in the bottom for extra water to drain out. An adult can easily add small holes to the bottom of a potential pot using a nail and hammer or a pair of scissors.

SIMPLE EXPLANATION

Plants are pretty special among living things because they are able to make their own food! They don't need to hunt or cook or go to the grocery store; instead they make their own meals in their leaves. To make their own food, plants need a few things: sunlight, air, water, and soil (dirt). Plants are very good at getting what they need and can grow their leaves toward sunlight and their roots toward water.

LONGER EXPLANATION

Plants can make their own food (a type of sugar called starch) through a process called photosynthesis. In their leaves, plants gather the things they need—water, nutrients from the soil, and carbon dioxide from the air—and use energy from the sun to make food.

In addition to food, photosynthesis also makes oxygen. Human beings and other animals breathe out carbon dioxide. We need to breathe in oxygen. Plants turn the carbon dioxide we breathe out into oxygen that we can breathe in during photosynthesis. They help us a lot that way!

SUPPLY LIST FOR THE ACTIVITIES IN THIS CHAPTER

- [ ] Ziplock bags
- [ ] Paper towels or cotton balls
- [ ] Plant pots, large cups, or large containers from your recycling
- [ ] Potting soil
- [ ] Seeds (recommend beans or peas)
- [ ] Tape
- [ ] Marker (for labeling)
- [ ] Cardboard box
- [ ] Pieces of cardboard or cardstock
- [ ] Food coloring or liquid watercolors
- [ ] Celery
- [ ] Plexiglass
- [ ] Plaster of paris

CHALLENGE: DESIGN A PLANT MAZE

Plants can grow to reach the things they need, like sunlight. Will your plant be able to grow through your maze and reach the light?

MISSION: Tape pieces of cardboard or paper inside a box to create a maze between the plant at the bottom of the box and the hole of light at the top.

MATERIALS

- [ ] Cardboard box with one hole at the top
- [ ] Sunny window
- [ ] Small bean sprout (a few inches tall)
- [ ] Pieces of cardboard or paper
- [ ] Tape

HELPFUL HINTS

- Be sure that the only light in the box is coming from the hole at the top. Patch any other holes in the box that would allow light in.
- Be sure to place the finished maze where it will get as much sunlight as possible.
- Create some sort of door or lid that is removable so you can check on the progress of your plant.
- Don't forget to regularly water your plant.

Extensions

CAN YOU DESIGN A MAZE THAT IS SO COMPLICATED YOUR PLANT CAN'T REACH SUNLIGHT BEFORE IT DIES?

HOW DOES THE SIZE OF YOUR BOX (FOR EXAMPLE, SMALL OR TALL) CHANGE WHETHER THE PLANT CAN REACH THE SUNLIGHT?

HOW DOES THE NUMBER OF TURNS IN THE MAZE CHANGE THE NUMBER OF DAYS IT TAKES FOR THE PLANT TO REACH THE LIGHT?

DO YOU THINK DIFFERENT TYPES OF PLANTS (FOR EXAMPLE, PEAS OR BEANS) DO A BETTER JOB OF MAKING IT THROUGH THE MAZE THAN OTHERS?

WHAT HAPPENS IF YOU HAVE MORE THAN ONE HOLE LETTING LIGHT IN?

EXPERIMENT: HOW DEEP SHOULD YOU PLANT A SEED TO GET THE BEST GROWTH?

Does it matter how deep you plant a seed? Is there such a thing as planting too deep? If you set a seed on top of the soil, will it still grow? Let's find out if there's a depth that is best.

MAKE YOUR GUESS: What depth do you think is the best for planting a seed?

THINGS TO CONSIDER WHEN RUNNING YOUR EXPERIMENT

Remember that the only thing you are changing is how deep you are burying the seeds. All other things (for example, how often they are watered and their exposure to sunlight) should stay the same!

- How many seeds will you use? What kind?
- What depths are you going to use?
- How long will you run the experiment?
- Be sure to water your seeds and to keep them near sunlight.

DATA

- How will you measure growth?
- How often will you check?

WHAT DID YOU LEARN FROM YOUR EXPERIMENT? WHAT HAPPENED? WHY DO YOU THINK IT HAPPENED?

CHLOE, AGE 4, AND LUKE, AGE 7, USED STRAWS TO POKE HOLES OF DIFFERENT DEPTHS IN A ROOT VIEWER (SEE PAGE 50 TO BUILD YOUR OWN) AND THEN THEY DROPPED ONE PINTO BEAN INTO EACH HOLE. THEY CHOSE TO MAKE SOME HOLES SHALLOW (INCLUDING ONE THAT WAS ON THE SURFACE), SOME MEDIUM, AND SEVERAL DEEP—AT THE BOTTOM OF THE ROOT VIEWER. ALL OF THE SEEDS SPROUTED, BUT THE SEEDS IN SHALLOW HOLES (WITHIN AN INCH OF THE TOP) GREW THE FASTEST.

ADVANCED LEVEL: What other questions do you have about plants and planting depth? Design an experiment to answer a question.

EXPLORE: COLLECT AND GROW
SEEDS FROM YOUR FOOD

There are all sorts of seeds in the fruits and vegetables you eat! Keep an eye out as you snack on fruit, or as you prepare vegetables for dinner, and gather several sample seeds to explore. When you are done examining them (and maybe even drawing a picture of them!), add them to a sprouting bag with a label. After they have sprouted, you can transfer them to soil with a label and watch them grow.

MATERIALS

- [ ] A variety of seeds
- [ ] Permanent marker
- [ ] Ziplock bag
- [ ] Paper towel
- [ ] Soil
- [ ] Cups

HELPFUL HINTS

- Don't worry if some of the seeds you use won't sprout.

Extensions

IF YOU HAD SEEDS THAT DIDN'T SPROUT, WHY DO YOU THINK THEY DIDN'T? CAN YOU DESIGN AN EXPERIMENT TO TEST ANY OF YOUR GUESSES?

WHICH SEEDS SPROUT THE FASTEST?

WHICH PLANTS GROW THE FASTEST?

DOES THE SIZE OF THE SEED TELL YOU ANYTHING ABOUT THE SIZE OF THE PLANT?

SET UP A MYSTERY SEED QUIZ AND SEE IF YOUR CHILD CAN GUESS WHICH PLANT IT BELONGS TO. TAKE A PAIR OF OLD SOCKS AND PUT THEM OVER YOUR SHOES. TAKE A WALK THROUGH A FIELD OR ANOTHER AREA WHERE THERE IS A LARGE VARIETY OF PLANT LIFE. HAVE AN ADULT CUT THE SOCKS OFF YOUR SHOES AND PLANT THEM IN A POT WITH SOIL. DO PLANTS GROW? IF YES, WHY DO YOU THINK IT MIGHT BE USEFUL FOR THE SEEDS TO BE ABLE TO HOLD ONTO YOUR SOCKS?

CHALLENGE: DESIGN A LEAF THAT WILL KEEP WATER FROM EVAPORATING

Plants grow all over the world in many different types of places—hot, cold, sandy, and salty. Some plants even grow underwater! Over time, changes to leaves, roots, and other parts have developed to help plants in all sorts of different environments get the things they need. These special changes, called adaptations, help them grow in challenging places, like deserts. What kinds of changes to a leaf would help a plant survive in a hot and dry place? Pretend you are making a leaf and see if you can find ways to keep ½ teaspoon of water on a paper towel from evaporating overnight.

MISSION: Make model (pretend) leaves by setting out several paper towel squares and adding ½ teaspoon of water to each of them. Try to keep them wet overnight by folding, wrapping, or whatever else you can think of, using the materials provided.

MATERIALS

- [ ] Paper towel squares
- [ ] ½ teaspoon of water
- [ ] Wax paper
- [ ] Plastic wrap
- [ ] Additional paper towels
- [ ] Paper
- [ ] Scissors
- [ ] Tape

HELPFUL HINTS

- Try as many different ideas and combinations as you can.
- Make sure all of your paper towel "leaves" are stored in the same place and wait 24 hours to check them.

Real-life application

IN THE DESERT AND OTHER DRY AREAS, PLANTS HAVE SEVERAL ADAPTATIONS FOR HOLDING ON TO THE WATER THEY GATHER. THEY OFTEN HAVE THICK LEAVES OR LEAVES WITH A WAXY COATING ON THEM. THEY ALSO HAVE ADDITIONAL WAYS TO STORE WATER SO THAT WHEN IT IS AVAILABLE, THEY GET AS MUCH AS POSSIBLE.

Extensions

TAKE A TRIP TO A GARDEN OR HOME IMPROVEMENT STORE AND LOOK AT THE INDOOR PLANTS. CAN YOU FIND PLANTS WITH THICK LEAVES? WHAT ABOUT LEAVES WITH WAXY COATINGS? HOW DO THESE TYPES OF LEAVES COMPARE TO THE PAPER TOWEL "LEAVES" YOU MADE? DO THEY GIVE YOU MORE IDEAS FOR HOW TO MAKE A PAPER TOWEL "LEAF"?

COMPARE HOW LONG IT TAKES A PLAIN PAPER TOWEL WITH 1/2 TEASPOON OF WATER LAID OUT FLAT TO DRY OUT TO HOW LONG IT TAKES YOUR BEST PAPER TOWEL "LEAF" TO DRY OUT.

EXPERIMENT: DO SEEDS SPROUT FASTER IF THEY ARE WARM OR COLD?

Is there a reason why we usually start our gardens in late spring? Do seeds grow differently if it's warm or cold, or will they grow no matter what the temperature is?

MAKE YOUR GUESS: Which do you think will grow seeds faster: warmer or cooler temperatures?

THINGS TO CONSIDER WHEN RUNNING YOUR EXPERIMENT:

Remember that the only thing you are changing is the temperature surrounding the seeds. All other things should stay the same!

- How many seeds will you use?
- What type of container will you use for your seeds?
- Where will you put the seeds to get different temperatures? (For example, by a heater vent, near the oven, outside, in the refrigerator, in the freezer, with a blanket around it—but be sure the blanket isn't blocking sunlight)
- Try to keep the amount of sunlight the seeds receive the same.

DATA

- How will you decide if the seeds are growing faster?
- Will you measure anything?
- How often will you check?

WHAT DID YOU LEARN FROM YOUR EXPERIMENT? WHAT HAPPENED? WHY DO YOU THINK IT HAPPENED?

Real-life application

MOST SEEDS REQUIRE WARM TEMPERATURES TO SPROUT AND GROW. YOU MIGHT NOTICE THAT PEOPLE START GARDENS IN SPRING AND SUMMER; THIS IS BECAUSE OF THE WARMER TEMPERATURES. THE TEMPERATURE A SEED NEEDS TO SPROUT DEPENDS ON THE KIND OF PLANT. IF YOU BUY A PACK OF SEEDS FOR YOUR GARDEN, YOU CAN FIND THE NEEDED TEMPERATURE PRINTED ON THE BACK.

SAMANTHA, AGE 5, CHOSE TO PLACE THREE BEANS IN EACH SPROUTING BAG. SHE PLACED ONE BAG JUST OUTSIDE THE SLIDING GLASS DOOR AND ONE ON THE INSIDE OF THE SLIDING GLASS DOOR; ONE IN THE KITCHEN OUTSIDE THE REFRIGERATOR AND ONE IN THE REFRIGERATOR; ONE ON THE CEILING OF HER ROOM AND ONE ON THE FLOOR OF HER ROOM. THE BEANS ON THE KITCHEN COUNTER SPROUTED FIRST (AFTER FOUR DAYS!). ONLY THE SEEDS IN WARM LOCATIONS SPROUTED.

ADVANCED LEVEL: What other questions do you have about seeds and temperature? Samantha wants to try her experiment again, but wants to know if several different types of seeds will do the same thing! Design an experiment to answer one of your questions (or Samantha's!).

EXPERIMENT: CAN YOU CHANGE THE COLOR OF PLANTS IF YOU SPROUT SEEDS IN COLORED WATER?

If you put cut white daisy flowers in colored water, their petals will change color. What happens if you water a seed with colored water? Will it grow into a plant with colored leaves?

MAKE YOUR GUESS: Do you think seeds sprouted in colored water will grow colored leaves?

THINGS TO CONSIDER WHEN RUNNING YOUR EXPERIMENT

Remember that the only thing you are changing is adding color to the water used to sprout the seeds. All other things should stay the same!

- How many seeds will you use?
- How many colors will you try?
- How many drops of food coloring will you add to make each color? How much water?
- Where will you place the seeds to grow?

DATA

- How will you decide if the color of the leaves is changing? (Hint: if you sprout seeds in clear water, you can compare them)
- How often will you check the seeds?

WHAT DID YOU LEARN FROM YOUR EXPERIMENT? WHAT HAPPENED? WHY DO YOU THINK IT HAPPENED?

SAMANTHA, AGE 5, TRIED SPROUTING LIMA BEANS WITH 2 TABLESPOONS OF WATER, 10 DROPS OF FOOD COLORING, AND COTTON BALLS. SHE WAITED TWO WEEKS AND HER BEANS DIDN'T SPROUT. SHE TRIED THE SAME EXPERIMENT IN A SPROUTING BAG AND NONE OF HER BEANS SPROUTED! SHE NOW WANTS TO KNOW IF A DIFFERENT TYPE OF SEED WILL SPROUT WITH FOOD COLORING.

ADVANCED LEVEL: What other questions do you have about water and seeds? Design an experiment to answer a question.

EXPLORE: MATCH THE SPROUTS WITH THE SEEDS

Gather a few different types (and sizes) of seeds and plant some of them. Once they have grown a few inches tall, compare them to each other and to the seeds they came from. Can you tell which seed belongs to which sprout? How are the roots different between the sprouts? Why do you think this is? How are the leaves different? Do larger seeds grow into larger sprouts?

MATERIALS

☐ Several different types of seeds (for example, radish, carrot, corn, bean, pea, marigold)

☐ Sprouting bags or pots with soil

HELPFUL HINTS

- If you plant all the seeds at the same time, you can compare how quickly they grow!
- Be sure to label the seeds you plant.

Extensions

WHAT OTHER QUESTIONS DO YOU HAVE ABOUT DIFFERENT TYPES OF SPROUTS?

EXPERIMENT: WHAT INGREDIENTS WILL CELERY MOVE TO ITS LEAVES?

Plants move water from the soil up to their leaves. What happens if we mix things like color or salt or sugar into the water? Will the plant move the things dissolved in water to its leaves? This is the only experiment in the book where you'll have a chance to taste-test if you wish!

MAKE YOUR GUESS: Which ingredients do you think celery will move to its leaves?

THINGS TO CONSIDER WHEN RUNNING YOUR EXPERIMENT

Remember that the only thing you are changing is what you are dissolving in the water with the celery. All other things should stay the same!

- How many stems of celery will you use?
- What ingredients will you dissolve in water (for example, food coloring, salt, sugar, extracts like peppermint, or anything else edible you can think of)? Have an adult double-check that the ingredients you add are safe to taste.
- How long will you run your experiment?

DATA

- How will you decide if the ingredients have moved to the leaves? (Hint: If you have regular celery, you could always do a taste-test and compare. Normally you wouldn't taste a science experiment, but this experiment is different!)
- How often will you check?

WHAT DID YOU LEARN FROM YOUR EXPERIMENT? WHAT HAPPENED? WHY DO YOU THINK IT HAPPENED?

Real-life application

PLANTS WON'T ABSORB EVERYTHING FROM THE SOIL INTO THEIR LEAVES, BUT CERTAIN PESTICIDES AND TOXINS CAN BE ABSORBED INTO FOODS. FARMERS NEED TO BE VERY CAREFUL ABOUT WHAT IS IN THE SOIL THEY PLANT THEIR CROPS IN.

MIA, AGE 5, TESTED CELERY IN 1 CUP OF WATER, 1 CUP OF WATER WITH 1 TABLESPOON OF SUGAR STIRRED IN, 1 CUP OF WATER WITH 6 DROPS OF PURPLE FOOD COLORING, 1 CUP OF WATER WITH A TEASPOON OF LEMON EXTRACT, AND 1 CUP OF WATER WITH A TEASPOON OF PEPPERMINT EXTRACT. AFTER 24 HOURS, SHE COULD SEE THE PURPLE IN THE CELERY LEAVES AND THOUGHT SHE COULD SMELL PEPPERMINT IN THE CRUSHED LEAVES, BUT SHE WASN'T SURE. SHE MIGHT HAVE ALSO TASTED LEMON, SUGAR, AND PEPPERMINT IN THE LEAVES.

ADVANCED LEVEL: What other questions do you have about celery? Design an experiment to answer a question.

EXPLORE: DISSECT PLANTS AND FLOWERS

Plants have parts that are perfect for the different things they need. Roots are big, long, and thin to gather water and vitamins (nutrients) from the soil; flowers are bright and pretty to attract bees and other pollinators; and leaves are large and green to gather the sunlight plants need to make their own food. Gather a few different plants (every type of plant is so different!) and take them apart to get a better look at what goes on inside the plants. Tape the different plant parts into your journal when you are done.

MATERIALS

☐ A variety of plants (some flowering)   ☐ Scissors   ☐ Tape

HELPFUL HINTS

- Weeds work really well for this activity, and older flower arrangements with a variety of flowers.

CHALLENGE: MAKE A PLANT GROW DOWN INSTEAD OF UP

Have you noticed that plant stems and leaves always grow up? Why is that? Can you make a plant's stems and leaves grow down instead?

MISSION: Design a way to get a sprouting seed to grow down. You can make changes as the plant starts to grow if you'd like. The goal is to make it always grow down.

MATERIALS: Sprouting seeds and anything else you can think of (for example, cups, plastic bags, paper towels)!

HELPFUL HINTS

- If you find that your plant is starting to grow up, change what you are doing and try something new!
- Be sure your plant is watered and has sunlight.

Extensions

TAKE A FULL-GROWN PLANT AND TURN IT UPSIDE DOWN (CREATE SOMETHING THAT WILL KEEP THE SOIL FROM SPILLING). LET IT GROW LIKE THIS FOR SEVERAL WEEKS. WHAT HAPPENS? WHY DO YOU THINK THIS HAPPENS?

EXPERIMENT: HOW MUCH WATER GROWS TALL PLANTS?

Plants need water to grow, but can you water them too much or too little? Let's find out how much water will make your plants grow the tallest.

MAKE YOUR GUESS: How much water do you think your plants will need to grow the tallest?

THINGS TO CONSIDER WHEN RUNNING YOUR EXPERIMENT

Remember that the only thing you are changing is the amount of water you are adding to your plants. All other things should stay the same!

- How many seeds or plants will you use?
- How much water will you add to each?
- How long will you run your experiment?
- Be sure to keep your plants near sunlight.

DATA

- How will you measure your plants? How often?

WHAT DID YOU LEARN FROM YOUR EXPERIMENT? WHAT HAPPENED? WHY DO YOU THINK IT HAPPENED?

Real-life application

DIFFERENT TYPES (SPECIES) OF PLANTS NEED DIFFERENT AMOUNTS OF WATER. SOME TYPES OF PLANTS ARE ABLE TO STORE WATER AND DON'T GROW AS WELL IN WET SOIL. OTHERS NEED DAMP SOIL AND LOTS OF WATER TO GROW. EACH TYPE OF PLANT HAS ADAPTATIONS (WAYS TO SURVIVE) IN THEIR NORMAL HABITAT (WHERE THEY GROW IN NATURE). PLANTS THAT GROW IN DESERTS NEED LESS WATER TO GROW WELL, BUT PLANTS IN BOGS AND RAINFORESTS NEED MORE.

ELSIE, AGE 6, DECIDED TO TRY 20 ML, 40 ML, 50 ML, 70 ML, AND 90 ML OF WATER EVERY OTHER DAY ON HER PINTO BEAN SEEDLINGS. SHE FOUND THAT THE BEANS WITH 40 ML, 50 ML, 70 ML, AND 90 ML OF WATER GREW THE TALLEST.

ADVANCED LEVEL: What other questions do you have about seeds and amounts of water? Design an experiment to answer a question.

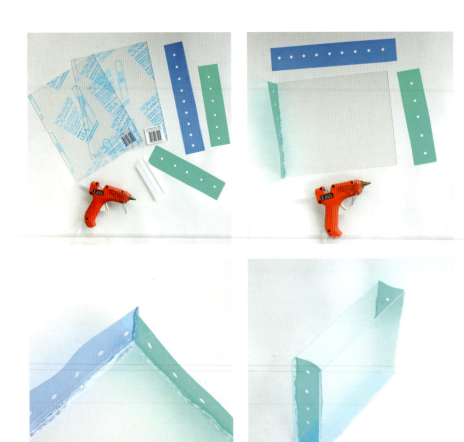

EXPLORE: MAKE YOUR OWN ROOT VIEWER

You can make your own root viewer to see how roots grow, how things decompose over time, or watch the interesting growth of bulbs or root vegetables.

MATERIALS

- [ ] Two 8-by-10-inch plexiglass sheets
- [ ] Hot glue gun that has a low heat setting
- [ ] Plastic binder dividers
- [ ] Scissors
- [ ] Hole punch

HELPFUL HINTS

- You can get plexiglass sheets from inexpensive picture frames, from a plexiglass store, or from a home improvement store. We bought ours from Home Depot (Plaskolite 8-by-10-inch polystyrene sheets).
- Plastic binder dividers can be purchased from an office supply store.

DIRECTIONS

1. Cut two 3-by-8-inch strips of plastic binder divider for each side of your root viewer and one 3-by-10-inch strip of plastic binder divider for the bottom of your root viewer.

2. Using a hole punch, punch three to four holes spaced out along the midline of the bottom 3-by-10-inch strip of plastic binder divider. (Alternatively, you can use a small drill to drill holes in the sides and bottom once the root viewer is constructed)

3. Lay one of your 8-by-10-inch plexiglass sheets flat and lay a line of hot glue (on the low heat setting) along one edge. Place a strip of plastic binder divider perpendicular to the plexiglass and hold while the glue dries. Reinforce the binder divider strip by laying a bead of hot glue on each side of the strip. Hold until it dries.

4. Repeat step 3 for each additional strip of plastic binder divider.

5. Add a seam of glue inside and outside each plastic binder corner.

6. Lay the other 8-by-10-inch plexiglass sheet flat and follow steps 3 and 4 until you have a completed root viewer.

7. Once the glue is dry, add potting soil and water.

8. Add seeds or plants.

9. Elevate them slightly (we placed them on two bottle caps, but placing them on upside-down cups would work too), so that air can circulate and water can drain.

EXPERIMENT: WILL PLANTS GROW IF YOU WATER THEM WITH JUICE OR ANOTHER LIQUID?

We always water plants with water, but do we have to? Will a plant grow just as well (or better!) with juice or milk?

MAKE YOUR GUESS: Do you think plants will grow or die if you use a liquid that isn't water?

THINGS TO CONSIDER WHEN RUNNING YOUR EXPERIMENT

Remember that the only thing you are changing is what liquid you use on the plants. All other things should stay the same!

- How many plants will you use?
- What liquids other than water will you use?
- How long will you do your experiment?
- Be sure to keep your plants where they will get some sunlight.

DATA

- How will you decide if the plants are growing like normal with liquids other than water?
- How often will you check?

WHAT DID YOU LEARN FROM YOUR EXPERIMENT? WHAT HAPPENED? WHY DO YOU THINK IT HAPPENED?

CHLOE, AGE 4, USED FOUR PEA PLANTS FOR HER EXPERIMENT. SHE WATERED ONE WITH 30 ML OF WATER EVERY OTHER DAY, ANOTHER WITH 30 ML OF LEMON JUICE EVERY OTHER DAY, ANOTHER WITH 30 ML OF MILK EVERY OTHER DAY, AND THE FINAL PLANT SHE WATERED WITH 30 ML OF CLUB SODA EVERY OTHER DAY. SHE FOUND THAT THE PLANT WATERED WITH CLUB SODA DIED TWO DAYS LATER. A FEW DAYS AFTER THAT, THE PLANT WATERED WITH LEMON JUICE DIED. THE PLANT WATERED WITH MILK HAD LOTS OF MOLD ON TOP OF THE SOIL, BUT IT WAS STILL GROWING WEEKS LATER, AS WAS THE PLANT WATERED WITH WATER.

ADVANCED LEVEL: What other questions do you have about watering and plants? Design an experiment to answer a question.

EXPERIMENT: CAN PLANTS GROW IN THE DARK?

You usually see plants outside or near a window if they are indoors. Do plants need to have sunlight to survive? What will plants look like after living in the dark for a few days or a few weeks?

MAKE YOUR GUESS: Do you think they will or won't continue to grow? How else do you think they will change?

THINGS TO CONSIDER WHEN RUNNING YOUR EXPERIMENT:
Remember that the only thing you are changing is the amount of light. All other things should stay the same!

- How many plants will you use?
- Will you try several completely dark places or just one?

- How long will you run the experiment?
- Be sure to regularly water your plants.

DATA

- How will you decide if the plants are still growing?
- Are there any other observations you want to write down?

WHAT DID YOU LEARN FROM YOUR EXPERIMENT? WHAT HAPPENED? WHY DO YOU THINK IT HAPPENED?

Real-life application

DIFFERENT PLANTS REQUIRE DIFFERENT AMOUNTS OF LIGHT. TAKE A TRIP TO A GARDEN STORE AND SEE IF YOU CAN FIND PLANTS THAT GROW IN SHADE. HOW ARE THEY DIFFERENT THAN PLANTS THAT NEED FULL SUN? WHAT DO YOU THINK THE PLANTS YOU EXPERIMENTED WITH NEED?

SAMANTHA, AGE 5, CHOSE TO USE FOUR PEA PLANTS FOR HER EXPERIMENT. SHE PLACED TWO PEA PLANTS INSIDE A LARGE BOX AND MADE SURE THAT ALL THE CORNERS AND EDGES WERE TAPED SO THEY WOULDN'T LET ANY LIGHT IN. SHE LEFT THE OTHER TWO PEA PLANTS IN THE WINDOW. SHE WATERED ALL THE PEA PLANTS EVERY OTHER NIGHT. THE PLANTS IN THE DARK BOX DIED AFTER A WEEK WITHOUT SUNLIGHT, BUT THE PLANTS IN THE WINDOW CONTINUED TO GROW.

ADVANCED LEVEL: What other questions do you have about plants and amount of light? Design an experiment to answer a question.

EXPERIMENT: CAN PLANTS CRACK PLASTER?

Just how strong are plants? If you place a layer of plaster over soil and plant a seed in the plaster, will the plant break free as it grows?

MAKE YOUR GUESS: Do you think growing plants can crack plaster?

THINGS TO CONSIDER WHEN RUNNING YOUR EXPERIMENT

Remember that the only thing you are changing is the amount of plaster you're adding. All other things should stay the same!

- How many seeds will you use? What kind?
- Follow the directions on your plaster of paris container to make the plaster. (A general rule of thumb is 2 parts plaster to every 1 part water.)

- How many different amounts of added plaster will you try?
- Be sure that your pots are placed near a source of sunlight and that they get regularly watered.

DATA

- How will you measure the thickness of the plaster?
- How will you decide if the plaster is cracked?

HELPFUL TIP

If the air in your home is very dry, you may find that the exposed plant roots dry out and the seeds die quickly. If this happens, I recommend placing the pots with seeds in large ziplock bags and sealing them to make miniature greenhouses. The increased humidity will preserve the exposed roots.

WHAT DID YOU LEARN FROM YOUR EXPERIMENT? WHAT HAPPENED? WHY DO YOU THINK IT HAPPENED?

Real-life application

THE NEXT TIME YOU ARE WALKING ON A SIDEWALK WITH TREES, SEE IF YOU CAN FIND EXAMPLES OF PLANTS THAT HAVE BROKEN THROUGH CONCRETE!

SAMANTHA, AGE 5, PLANTED TWO PINTO BEANS IN SOIL, TWO PINTO BEANS IN 3 TEASPOONS OF PLASTER, TWO PINTO BEANS IN 5 TEASPOONS OF PLASTER, AND TWO PINTO BEANS IN 8 TEASPOONS OF PLASTER, AND KEPT THEM ALL IN A GREENHOUSE. SHE DYED THE PLASTER PINK BY ADDING FOOD COLORING TO IT. SHE FOUND THAT THE BEANS IN THE SOIL GREW FIRST. THE BEANS IN THE PLASTER POPPED OUT AND SENT ROOTS OUT ALONG THE TOP OF THE PLASTER. THE BEANS IN 5 TEASPOONS OF PLASTER AND 8 TEASPOONS OF PLASTER HAD ROOTS THAT FOUND SOIL AND GREW JUST AS TALL AS THE BEANS IN SOIL. THE BEANS IN 3 TEASPOONS OF PLASTER DIED AND NEVER GREW LEAVES.

ADVANCED LEVEL: What other questions do you have about plant strength? Design an experiment to answer a question.

EXPERIMENT: IF YOU COLOR PLANT LEAVES WITH A PERMANENT MARKER, WILL THE PLANTS STILL GROW?

Have you ever wanted to color a plant? This experiment is your chance! This question comes from one of our 6-year-old scientists, Elsie!

MAKE YOUR GUESS: Do you think your plant will still grow with permanent marker-colored leaves?

THINGS TO CONSIDER WHEN RUNNING YOUR EXPERIMENT

Remember that the only thing you are changing is coloring the plant leaves with permanent marker. All other things should stay the same!

- How many plants will you use?
- What color permanent marker will you use?
- Remember to place your plants where they will receive sunlight and to water them regularly.
- Will you color one side or both sides of the leaves?

DATA

- How will you decide if the plants with marker-colored leaves are growing the same, better, or worse than plants with uncolored leaves?
- Will you measure anything?
- How often will you check?

WHAT DID YOU LEARN FROM YOUR EXPERIMENT? WHAT HAPPENED? WHY DO YOU THINK IT HAPPENED?

ELSIE, AGE 6, CHOSE TWO PLANTS AND COLORED THE TOPS OF ALL THE LEAVES OF ONE PLANT WITH A PERMANENT MARKER AND LEFT A SECOND PLANT UNCOLORED. SHE FOUND THAT A FEW OF THE COLORED LEAVES TOWARD THE BOTTOM OF THE PLANT SHRIVELED, BUT THAT THE PLANT CONTINUED TO GROW!

ADVANCED LEVEL: What other questions do you have about plants and changing the color of their leaves? Design an experiment to answer a question.

Chapter 2
Water and Ice

INTRODUCTION

Did you know that the water on Earth today is the same water that was here when the dinosaurs were alive? And did you know that water is necessary for life? Water is a pretty important chemical.

SIMPLE EXPLANATION

Water is a liquid, which means it can take on the shape of any container you add it to. When water reaches a certain temperature (32 degrees Fahrenheit), it freezes or turns into a solid. We call the solid form of water ice. You can melt ice and turn it back into water.

The smallest bit of water is called a molecule. It's so small we can't even see it! Water molecules stick together and this helps water move. Water can climb up tree roots and up bits of paper because of this "stickiness."

LONGER EXPLANATION

Water can be a solid, a liquid, or a gas. If you lower the temperature of water to 32 degrees Fahrenheit or lower, it will become solid ice. If you raise the temperature of water to 100 degrees Fahrenheit or higher, it will boil and seem to disappear. The water doesn't actually disappear, but it becomes an invisible gas (water vapor). Water always freezes and evaporates at the same temperatures (unless you are up very high in the mountains, which can change the boiling point a bit).

Water is constantly being recycled through a process called the water cycle. Water evaporates (this means it turns into a gas, called water vapor) and goes up into clouds where it condenses (becomes a liquid droplet) and eventually precipitates (falls back down to the ground from the clouds) as rain, snow, or hail.

The smallest unit of water is called a molecule. It's very, very small. There are about 100 quintillion molecules of water in one water droplet! Water molecules are attracted to each other in the same way that your hair is sometimes attracted to a balloon. This attraction is what allows water to climb up tree roots to the tops of tall trees, and what helps water climb up paper and fabric.

SUPPLY LIST FOR THE ACTIVITIES IN THIS CHAPTER

- [ ] Salt
- [ ] Sugar
- [ ] Vinegar
- [ ] Cooking oil
- [ ] Water
- [ ] Foil
- [ ] Styrofoam (optional)
- [ ] Cotton balls
- [ ] Paper towels
- [ ] Tape
- [ ] Different types of paper (for example, cardstock, coffee filters, paper towels, tissue paper, computer paper, construction paper, watercolor paper)
- [ ] Dish soap
- [ ] Corn syrup
- [ ] Food coloring or liquid watercolors
- [ ] Cups or beakers
- [ ] Pennies
- [ ] Stopwatch
- [ ] Measuring cups and spoons
- [ ] Pipettes

CHALLENGE: MAKE ICE MELT FASTER

Which ingredient will melt ice the fastest? Or does ice always melt at the same speed?

MISSION: See if adding ingredients to ice will make it melt faster!

MATERIALS: Any ingredients from your house (for example, salt, sugar, cooking oil, hand sanitizer, water, and vinegar).

HELPFUL HINTS

- For added fun, freeze a small toy or other object (for example, a coin, bead, or paper clip) in an ice cube. Try to use the same sized pieces of ice for each ingredient you try.
- If you have a stopwatch, use it to measure how long it takes the ice to melt.
- If you measure how long it takes an ice cube to melt by itself with no ingredients, you can compare times to see if any of your methods are faster!

Real-life application

IN THE WINTER, PEOPLE OFTEN USE SALT OR SAND ON ICY SIDEWALKS AND ROADS. DID YOU TRY THESE INGREDIENTS ON YOUR ICE? WHAT HAPPENS TO ICE WHEN YOU USE THEM? WHY DO YOU THINK CITIES USE THESE INGREDIENTS?

EXPERIMENT: DOES THE SHAPE OF ICE CHANGE HOW FAST IT MELTS?

Will a long, thin piece of ice melt as fast as a cube shape? Or does all ice take the same amount of time to melt, no matter what the shape is?

MAKE YOUR GUESS: Do you think the shape of ice will change how quickly it will melt?

THINGS TO CONSIDER WHEN RUNNING YOUR EXPERIMENT

Remember that the only thing you are changing is the shape of the ice. All other things should stay the same!

- Remember to use the same amount of water each time.
- How will you make different shapes of ice? (Hint: using foil to make shapes works well)
- How long will you run your experiment?
- How many different shapes of ice will you use?

DATA

- What will you be measuring?

WHAT DID YOU LEARN FROM YOUR EXPERIMENT? WHAT HAPPENED? WHY DO YOU THINK IT HAPPENED?

Real-life application

THE NEXT TIME YOU NEED TO KEEP SOMETHING FROM MELTING FOR LONGER, COULD YOU APPLY WHAT YOU LEARNED HERE?

MIA, AGE 5, FROZE 1/2 A CUP OF BLUE COLORED WATER IN EACH OF FOUR DIFFERENT SHAPED PLASTIC CONTAINERS. SHE WAS SURPRISED TO FIND THAT THE ICE IN THE SHALLOW CONTAINER (THE THINNEST ICE) MELTED THE FASTEST.

ADVANCED LEVEL: What other questions do you have about shapes and melting times? Design an experiment to answer a question.

CHALLENGE: KEEP ICE FROM MELTING

Often we need to keep food frozen to keep it fresh. Using materials from around your house, can you create a cup that would keep ice frozen for as long as possible?

MISSION: Keep your ice cube from melting!

MATERIALS: Any ingredients from your house (for example, Styrofoam, cotton balls, foil, paper, large plastic cups, plastic wrap, towels, paper towels, tape, rubber bands, and anything else you can think of!).

HELPFUL HINTS

- The size of your ice will determine the length of your tests. Try half an ice cube for faster results (and remember to use a same sized ice cube each time!).
- Use a stopwatch to record the time it takes the ice cube to melt.

- Try out several different designs.
- You can place materials in your cup with your ice cube or around the outside of the cup.

Real-life application

HOW DO WE INSULATE THINGS TO KEEP THEM COLD? TAKE A LOOK AT VARIOUS COOLERS (IF YOU DON'T HAVE ANY, A GROCERY STORE OR SUPERSTORE SHOULD HAVE A VARIETY). HOW DO THESE COMPARE TO THE CUPS YOU DESIGNED? ARE THERE SIMILARITIES? DO YOU HAVE ANY MORE IDEAS FOR HOW TO BUILD A CUP AFTER LOOKING AT THE REAL-LIFE COOLERS?

THE NEXT TIME YOU GET GROCERIES, WATCH HOW YOUR FROZEN ITEMS ARE PACKED. DOES THIS GIVE YOU ANY MORE IDEAS FOR THINGS TO TRY?

Extensions

DOES YOUR MOST SUCCESSFUL CUP DESIGN ALSO WORK TO KEEP SOMETHING WARM? HAVE AN ADULT ADD SOME WARM OR HOT WATER TO TWO ZIPLOCK BAGS (REMEMBER TO ADD THE SAME AMOUNT OF WATER EACH TIME!) AND PLACE ONE FLAT AND PLACE THE OTHER IN YOUR CUP. WHICH ONE STAYS WARM FOR THE LONGEST? IF YOU HAVE A THERMOMETER AND STOPWATCH, CAN YOU MEASURE THE TIMES AND TEMPERATURES TO COMPARE THEM?

EXPERIMENT: WHAT KIND OF PAPER FLOWER OPENS THE FASTEST?

Does the type of paper you use change the speed at which a paper flower will open?

MAKE YOUR GUESS: Which kind of paper flower do you think will open the fastest?

DIRECTIONS FOR MAKING FOLDED PAPER FLOWERS

1. Draw a large flower with several petals on cardstock or cardboard, cut it out, and use it as a template (you can use your template in the experiment after you're done with it!).
2. Trace your flower template on to several different kinds of paper.
3. Fold one petal in at a time until all petals are folded in, as pictured above.
4. Place your folded flower petals up in water and watch them unfold!

THINGS TO CONSIDER WHEN RUNNING YOUR EXPERIMENT

Remember that the only thing you are changing is the type of paper used. All other things should stay the same!

- Remember to use same sized flowers each time and to fold them the same way each time.
- What kinds of paper are you going to use (for example, computer paper, construction paper, cardstock, wax paper, paper towels, newspaper, grocery bag paper)?
- How many times will you try each kind of paper flower?

DATA

- How will you measure how long it takes the paper flowers to open?

WHAT DID YOU LEARN FROM YOUR EXPERIMENT? WHAT HAPPENED? WHY DO YOU THINK IT HAPPENED?

Real-life application

REAL FLOWERS OPEN WHEN PLANTS MOVE WATER INTO THE PETALS! PLANTS ARE ABLE TO QUICKLY MOVE WATER TO THEIR DIFFERENT PARTS, SUCH AS THEIR FLOWER PETALS OR LEAVES. PAPER THAT IS ABLE TO MOVE WATER QUICKLY WILL CREATE THE FASTEST OPENING FLOWERS.

SAMANTHA, AGE 5, TRIED WAX PAPER, ORIGAMI PAPER, CONSTRUCTION PAPER, AND CARDSTOCK PAPER FLOWERS. SHE FOUND THAT THE CONSTRUCTION PAPER FLOWERS OPENED FASTEST.

CHALLENGE: CREATE A LONG-LASTING BUBBLE SOLUTION

Can you make a bubble solution that creates long-lasting bubbles? How long will your bubbles last without popping?

MISSION: Develop a recipe for long-lasting bubbles.

MATERIALS

- [ ] Dish soap (Joy or Dawn are recommended)
- [ ] G__erin (optional)
- [ ] W__
- [ ] Corn syrup
- [ ] Bubble wands
- [ ] Cups
- [ ] Various measuring spoons

HELPFUL HINTS

- Be sure to write down your recipes. If you come up with a good one, you might want to make it again and it's useful to keep track of what isn't working well.
- If you have a stopwatch, measure how long your bubbles last in seconds.
- Try several different combinations of ingredients.
- You may want to wear goggles to keep bubbles away from your eyes.

Extensions

CAN YOU FIND A SOLUTION THAT MAKES THE BIGGEST POSSIBLE BUBBLES? IS IT DIFFERENT THAN THE SOLUTION NEEDED TO MAKE THE LONGEST-LASTING BUBBLES?

EXPERIMENT: WHAT KIND OF PAPER MAKES A RAINBOW THE FASTEST?

If you place part of a paper towel in a cup of colored water (and let the other part of it hang over the edge), the water will "walk" up the paper towel over the edge of the cup. You can then catch the drips in an empty cup. Try using more cups with the colors red, yellow, and blue, and catch the drips in empty cups between them. This "walking" water will mix colors in the empty cups and make a pretty rainbow after several hours. What happens if you change the type of paper? Will the water still "walk" at the same speed and make a rainbow in the same amount of time?

MAKE YOUR GUESS: Which type of paper will create the fastest rainbow?

THINGS TO CONSIDER WHEN RUNNING YOUR EXPERIMENT

Remember that the only thing you are changing is the type of paper used between cups. All other things should stay the same!

- Remember to use the same amount of water and the same sized cups and the same amount of each kind of paper.
- The initial setup should include six cups placed in a circle—one for each red, yellow, and blue colored waters and empty cups between them. Place part of your paper in an empty cup and fold it so that the other part is touching colored water

in another cup. You can use a few drops of food coloring to color the red, yellow, and blue water (use the same amount each time!).

- What types of paper will you use (for example, paper towels, toilet paper, filter paper, tissues, tissue paper, and computer paper)?

DATA

- How will you measure the amounts of water per cup?
- How will you measure how long it takes (remember it may take several hours)?

WHAT DID YOU LEARN FROM YOUR EXPERIMENT? WHAT HAPPENED? WHY DO YOU THINK IT HAPPENED?

Real-life application

PLANT ROOTS HAVE ADAPTATIONS THAT MAKE THEM VERY GOOD AT QUICKLY MOVING WATER. SOME PAPERS ARE DESIGNED TO ABSORB WATER WELL, AND OTHERS ARE MADE TO REPEL WATER. PAPER THAT HAS A DESIGN SIMILAR TO PLANT ROOTS WILL BE ABLE TO MOVE WATER QUICKLY.

AMELIA, AGE 4, AND ROBBY, AGE 4, TESTED TOILET PAPER, FACIAL TISSUES, WAX PAPER, COMPUTER PAPER, AND PAPER TOWELS. THEY FOUND THAT THE PAPER TOWEL MADE A RAINBOW THE FASTEST. THE FACIAL TISSUE MOVED A SMALL AMOUNT OF WATER, BUT DIDN'T MAKE A COMPLETE RAINBOW. THE TOILET PAPER DISINTEGRATED AND THE WAX AND COMPUTER PAPER DIDN'T MOVE ANY WATER AT ALL!

EXPLORE: PAINT ON DAMP AND DRY PAPER TOWELS AND WATCH THE COLOR SPREAD

Explore how water changes the spread of color and make some art! Dampen one paper towel (it should be wet, but not dripping) and place it next to (but not touching) a dry paper towel. Using a pipette, add colors to each side and notice the difference in how the color spreads. You can make watercolors to paint with either by adding 5 drops of food coloring to 1 teaspoon water or by using liquid watercolors.

MATERIALS

☐ Damp and dry paper towels   ☐ Tray   ☐ Watercolors   ☐ Pipette

HELPFUL HINTS

- Make sure your damp and dry paper towels aren't touching.
- Place the paper towels on a cookie sheet or in another container to catch any spills.

Extensions

DO YOU SEE THE SAME THING HAPPEN WHEN YOU PAINT DAMP AND DRY PAPER?

WHAT DO YOU THINK IS HAPPENING?

PLANTS ABSORB NUTRIENTS THEY NEED FROM THE SOIL WITH THEIR ROOTS. WHY DO YOU THINK PLANT ROOTS ARE USUALLY MORE SUCCESSFUL IN DAMP SOIL?

EXPLORE: FIT AS MANY DROPS OF WATER AS YOU CAN ON A PENNY

This activity is a fun way to explore the properties of water and practice your pipette skills. Take a clean penny and add 1 drop of water at a time. How many drops can you fit on it? What techniques work best at getting the most water to stay on your penny?

MATERIALS

☐ Pipette   ☐ Penny   ☐ Cup of water   ☐ Dish soap

HELPFUL HINTS

- Try a variety of techniques (for example, fast or slow, pipette high above the penny and low down by the penny) to get the maximum number of water drops on your penny.

Extensions

TRY THE SAME THING WITH OTHER SURFACES. WHICH SURFACES WORK BEST? WHY DO YOU THINK THIS IS?

WHAT HAPPENS IF YOU ADD SOAP TO THE WATER ON YOUR PENNY? CAN YOU STILL GET THE SAME NUMBER OF DROPS TO STAY ON YOUR PENNY? WHY DO YOU THINK THIS IS?

CAN YOU FIT THE SAME NUMBER OF DROPS OF OTHER LIQUIDS (LIKE COOKING OIL OR VINEGAR) ON YOUR PENNY?

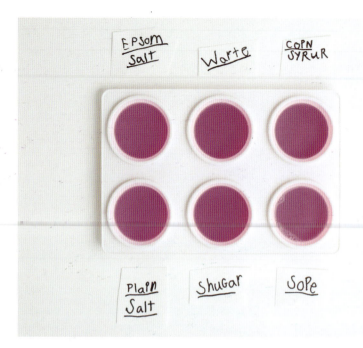

EXPERIMENT: CAN YOU CHANGE HOW LONG IT TAKES TO FREEZE WATER?

What happens if you mix ingredients in to water? Will it change how long it takes the water to freeze? Is there an ingredient you could add to water that would keep it from freezing in your freezer?

MAKE YOUR GUESS: Do you think adding kitchen ingredients to water will change how long it takes the water to freeze?

THINGS TO CONSIDER WHEN RUNNING YOUR EXPERIMENT

Remember that the only thing you are changing is that you are adding kitchen ingredients to water. All other things should stay the same!

- Remember to use the same amount of water each time.
- What ingredients will you use? How much of each? How much water?
- How long will you run your experiment?

DATA

- How will you measure how long it takes the water to freeze?
- How often will you check?

WHAT DID YOU LEARN FROM YOUR EXPERIMENT? WHAT HAPPENED? WHY DO YOU THINK IT HAPPENED?

Real-life application

WHY DO YOU THINK PEOPLE SOMETIMES ADD SALT TO THEIR FROZEN DRIVEWAYS AND SIDEWALKS IN THE WINTER?

WHAT WOULD HAPPEN IF YOU ADDED MUCH MORE OF EACH OF THE INGREDIENTS YOU TRIED? WOULD IT TAKE THE SAME AMOUNT OF TIME TO FREEZE?

ROSA, AGE 8, USED A TRAY OF CUPS FILLED WITH PINK COLORED WATER. ONE CUP HAD ONLY WATER, AND IN EACH OF THE OTHER CUPS, SHE ADDED 1 TEASPOON OF EPSOM SALT, 1 TEASPOON OF TABLE SALT, 1/4 TEASPOON OF DISH SOAP, 1/2 TEASPOON OF SUGAR, AND 1 TEASPOON OF CORN SYRUP. THE PLAIN WATER FROZE FIRST, FOLLOWED BY THE SOAPY WATER AND THE EPSOM SALT WATER. ALL OF THE WATER EVENTUALLY FROZE.

ADVANCED LEVEL: What other questions do you have about freezing water? Design an experiment to answer a question.

Chapter 3

Mold, Bacteria, and Fungus

INTRODUCTION

Bacteria and fungus might seem gross at first glance, but they are fascinating living things that help our world work! Because they are just about everywhere on Earth, it's very easy to find some to work with. Even within the walls of your house, you'll find that you have several different types of each. Though there are plenty of helpful bacteria and fungus, some are harmful. Because of this, you should not touch any of the bacteria or mold you grow in these experiments. To be safe, please use tape to seal the lids of petri dishes or seal your experiments in clear ziplock bags.

Please note that with the increase of both antibiotic-resistant bacteria and mold allergies, the experiments in this chapter should always involve parental supervision. Parents: Experiments must remain sealed and children should not directly touch, taste, or otherwise manipulate ongoing bacteria or mold experiments. Once the experiments have been set up, please seal them and place them out of reach of children. Please allow only your children to observe the growth or changes while you are directly supervising them. Do not reuse petri dishes or ziplock bags. Children and adults should always wash their hands well with soap and water after all of the activities in this chapter.

SIMPLE EXPLANATION

The most important job that bacteria and fungus have is breaking down dead things into dirt. When they do this, they make all the parts of the dead thing usable again. If you have compost at home or at school, bacteria and fungus are the ones working hard to turn your old food garbage into healthy soil for plants to grow. Bacteria and fungus are also used in making food, such as buttermilk, cheese, and bread! Bacteria and fungus can be found just about everywhere on Earth: in really hot or cold places, at the top of the highest mountains, and even under the sea on the ocean floor.

LONGER EXPLANATION

Bacteria and fungus work hard to break down once-living things (like a banana peel) into soil that is rich in nutrients that plants need to grow. Animals and weather can only do so much to break things down. We need bacteria and fungus to do the rest!

Though some bacteria and fungus cause disease, some prevent it! Many of the antibiotics we take when we are really sick are made from certain helpful kinds of bacteria and fungus.

Bacteria and fungus also help animals, like humans, break down and digest their food. There are bacteria that live in your intestines that help keep you healthy!

BASIC NUTRIENT AGAR RECIPE

Bacteria (and fungus) are like people—they like to eat certain things. This recipe will grow a wide variety of bacteria, but not all bacteria will grow on it. This means that there are lots more bacteria that aren't showing up.

It takes two animals to make a baby, but bacteria do something different. A single bacteria can grow and then split itself into two new bacteria. Then those two bacteria grow and each split to make four bacteria. This type of growth means that you can make a lot of bacteria very quickly. Some types of bacteria only take 20 minutes to split themselves in half. That means that if you have one million bacteria, in 20 minutes, you'll have about two million bacteria! Bacteria are so tiny that we can't see them without the help of very strong microscopes. But if you get enough bacteria growing in one spot, you will be able to see a little circular dot without a microscope. The little dot you see actually represents millions of bacteria! When you make your agar plates (petri dishes or cups with a thin layer of agar on the bottom), you'll need to wait two or three days before you'll see anything. This is because you are waiting for the bacteria to grow and split enough times that you can finally see them. Each dot on your agar plate represents one bacteria that grew and split thousands of times and is now a giant pile of bacteria!

To make nutrient agar (what you put in petri dishes or cups for bacteria to eat and grow on), you'll need:

- [ ] 2 ½ teaspoons of sugar
- [ ] 2 ½ tablespoons of agar powder
- [ ] 2 cups of low sodium beef broth
- [ ] 2 cups of water

Add all of your ingredients to a pot and have an adult stir with heat on medium-high until the mixture boils. Once it boils, have an adult remove it from the heat and let it cool down for 3 minutes. When the mixture has cooled for 3 minutes, have an adult pour a thin layer of agar into your petri dishes or into the bottom of a plastic cup. Allow the cups or petri dishes to cool in the refrigerator for two to three hours. When they are cool, put the lids on the petri dishes or cover the cups with plastic wrap. Store the agar plates in the refrigerator until you are ready to use them.

ADDING BACTERIA TO THE AGAR IN YOUR PETRI DISH OR CUP

You will be using a damp cotton swab to collect bacteria. Take the damp cotton swab and rub it across whatever surface you want to test. Then take the cotton swab and gently swish it across the surface of the agar. Agar is firm, but you can poke through it if you push hard. Bacteria will grow anywhere in or on agar, but if you poke through the smooth surface, you won't grow a nice round circle of bacteria to look at (it will look more like a cloudy clump). For the best results, very gently swish your cotton swab over the surface of the agar rather than pushing it down into the agar (dampening your cotton swab before using it will help it glide more smoothly over the surface of the agar). Be sure to use a new cotton swab each time you swab a new place you think there might be bacteria so you don't mix up the bacteria. And be sure to label your plates with the location you swabbed. Seal the plates around the edges with tape and let your plates sit somewhere warm and dry and that is out of reach of small children. In three to four days you should begin to see little dots of bacteria! Fungus will also grow on agar, and it looks very fuzzy and not circular. On your plates you will likely see a mix of both.

SUPPLY LIST FOR THE ACTIVITIES IN THIS CHAPTER

- [ ] Bread (with and without preservatives)
- [ ] Ziplock bags
- [ ] Sugar
- [ ] Petri dishes (you can substitute plastic cups if you'd rather not buy petri dishes online at a site like Amazon)
- [ ] Non-iodized salt
- [ ] Agar powder (this is like a firmer type of gelatin you can buy at some grocery stores and online at a site like Amazon)
- [ ] Beef broth
- [ ] Food coloring or liquid watercolors
- [ ] Tape
- [ ] Cotton swabs (such as Q-tips)
- [ ] Lemon juice
- [ ] Vinegar
- [ ] Soap
- [ ] Dry active yeast
- [ ] Balloons
- [ ] Banana
- [ ] Different types of food from your kitchen or pantry
- [ ] Measuring cups and spoons

EXPLORE: FIND BACTERIA

What sorts of bacteria can you find in your home? What sorts of bacteria can you find on you? Where do you think you'll find the most bacteria? Using agar plates prepared according to the recipe and directions found on page 80, explore your house and yourself and see what bacteria grows!

MATERIALS

☐ Agar plates (see page 82)   ☐ Cotton swabs   ☐ Tape

HELPFUL HINTS

- Practice your techniques using the activity on page 83.
- Try testing at least one place you think has no bacteria.
- Be sure to seal the edges of your agar plates with tape once you've swabbed them.
- Be sure to keep this experiment out of the reach of small children.

Extensions

WHAT ABOUT YOUR BACKYARD? DO YOU THINK YOU'LL FIND MORE OR LESS BACTERIA THERE?

DO YOU NOTICE ANY DIFFERENCE IN THE SHAPE, COLOR, OR SIZE OF THE DIFFERENT BACTERIA COLONIES?

ARE THERE PLACES WITH MORE MOLD THAN BACTERIA? WHY DO YOU THINK THIS IS?

EXPERIMENT: DO PRESERVATIVES CHANGE HOW FAST BREAD MOLDS?

A preservative is a chemical that is added to something to keep bacteria and mold from growing and breaking it down. Most store-bought foods have preservatives added to them. Do preservatives make a big difference in how long things last? Let's find out!

MAKE YOUR GUESS: Do you think adding preservatives to bread will change how long it takes to mold?

THINGS TO CONSIDER WHEN RUNNING YOUR EXPERIMENT

Remember that the only thing you are changing is whether the bread has preservatives. All other things should stay the same!

- Use a bread slice that is the same size and try to pick bread that was made around the same time (same freshness).
- Most store-bought breads contain preservatives; read the ingredient label to check.
- If you wish to make your own preservative-free bread, you can find a simple bread recipe on page 102.
- Be sure to keep this experiment out of the reach of small children.

DATA

- How will you store the bread? (Hint: for safety reasons, be sure to seal it so the mold isn't exposed)
- How will you measure the amount of mold?
- How often will you check?

WHAT DID YOU LEARN FROM YOUR EXPERIMENT? WHAT HAPPENED? WHY DO YOU THINK IT HAPPENED?

Real-life application

WHY DO YOU THINK MOST STORE-BOUGHT FOODS CONTAIN PRESERVATIVES?

SAMANTHA, AGE 5, PLACED A RECTANGLE OF HOMEMADE BREAD IN A ZIPLOCK BAG AND A RECTANGLE OF STORE-BOUGHT BREAD WITH PRESERVATIVES ADDED TO ANOTHER ZIPLOCK BAG. SHE PLACED BOTH BAGS IN A WINDOW. AFTER THREE DAYS, THE HOMEMADE BREAD STARTED TO MOLD, AND AFTER EIGHT DAYS, IT WAS COMPLETELY COVERED WITH MOLD ON EVERY SURFACE. THE STORE-BOUGHT BREAD WITH PRESERVATIVES HAD NO MOLD, BUT FELT STIFF AND STALE WHEN POKED THROUGH THE BAG.

ADVANCED LEVEL: What other questions do you have about preservatives and molding times? Design an experiment to answer a question.

EXPERIMENT: DOES COLORING THE AGAR CHANGE HOW BACTERIA GROW?

Agar plates for bacteria are usually uncolored. What happens if we add food coloring? Will the bacteria grow the same? Will it be colored?

MAKE YOUR GUESS: Do you think adding color to the agar will change anything about the bacterial growth? How?

THINGS TO CONSIDER WHEN RUNNING YOUR EXPERIMENT:

Remember that the only thing you are changing is whether color is added to the agar. All other things should stay the same, including where you get bacteria samples from!

- How many drops of food coloring will you use?
- Will you try more than one color?
- Seal the edges of your agar plates with tape once you've swabbed them.
- Be sure to keep this experiment out of the reach of small children.

DATA

- How will you measure any differences? (Hint: if you have an uncolored agar plate, it will be much easier to compare differences)
- How often will you check?

WHAT DID YOU LEARN FROM YOUR EXPERIMENT? WHAT HAPPENED? WHY DO YOU THINK IT HAPPENED?

SAMANTHA, AGE 5, SWABBED THE BOTTOM OF HER BROTHER'S SHOES EACH TIME. SHE FOUND THAT THE BACTERIA AND MOLD GREW MORE SLOWLY ON THE COLORED AGAR, ESPECIALLY ON THE PURPLE AGAR. THERE ALSO SEEMED TO BE FEWER KINDS OF BACTERIA ON THE COLORED AGAR PLATES.

ADVANCED LEVEL: What other questions do you have about color and bacteria? Design an experiment to answer a question.

EXPERIMENT: HOW WELL DOES YOUR HAND SANITIZER WORK?

Though our skin is covered with lots of harmless bacteria, it's possible to pick up harmful bacteria or viruses during our day when we touch a lot of surfaces. A lot of people use hand sanitizer because it's often easier than finding a place to wash your hands. Do you use hand sanitizer when you are out of the house? What about at school or daycare? Have you ever wondered how well it works? Here's your chance to find out!

MAKE YOUR GUESS: Do you think your hand sanitizer works well enough to kill the bacteria on your hands?

THINGS TO CONSIDER WHEN RUNNING YOUR EXPERIMENT

Remember that the only thing you are changing is whether you are adding hand sanitizer. Everything else should stay the same!

- If you're trying different sanitizers or different amounts of a sanitizer, be sure to touch some things in your house that you normally touch every day (for example, your dining room table, your couch, your kitchen counter) in between each experiment.
- How many agar plates will you need to prepare? (see page 80 for how to make agar plates)
- Hint: It's easiest to measure how well the hand sanitizer works if you have a plate with no hand sanitizer to compare it to.
- Seal the edges of your agar plates with tape once you've swabbed them.
- Be sure to keep this experiment out of the reach of small children.

DATA

- How will you measure the amount of bacteria on each agar plate?
- How often will you check?

WHAT DID YOU LEARN FROM YOUR EXPERIMENT? WHAT HAPPENED? WHY DO YOU THINK IT HAPPENED?

Extensions

TRY SEVERAL DIFFERENT BRANDS OR TYPES OF SANITIZERS. DO SOME WORK BETTER THAN OTHERS?

SAMANTHA, AGE 5, DECIDED TO TRY HER SPRAY HAND SANITIZER. SHE TOUCHED THE GROUND AND THEN AN AGAR PLATE AND THEN TOUCHED THE SAME AREA AGAIN AND SPRAYED THE HAND SANITIZER THREE TIMES AND RUBBED IT OVER HER HANDS. SHE FOUND THAT THE HAND SANITIZER DID KILL SOME OF THE BACTERIA, BUT NOT ALL OF IT. SHE NOW WANTS TO KNOW IF DIFFERENT AMOUNTS OF THE HAND SANITIZER (MORE OR LESS SPRAYS THAN SHE TRIED) WILL MAKE A DIFFERENCE IN THE AMOUNT OF BACTERIA ON HER HANDS.

ADVANCED LEVEL: What other questions do you have about bacteria and hand sanitizer? Design an experiment to answer a question (or Samantha's)!

CHALLENGE: KEEP CHICKEN STOCK FROM GROWING MOLD OR BACTERIA

Can you stop bacteria and mold from growing in a liquid that is just perfect for them? Growing bacteria and mold will make your liquid cloudy. Use ingredients from your kitchen and see what works best to keep your liquid clear!

MISSION: Keep the bacteria and mold from growing. The more bacteria and molds there are, the cloudier the chicken stock will get. Keep your chicken stock as clear as possible.

MATERIALS

☐ Cups	☐ Lemon juice	☐ Hand sanitizer
☐ Tape	☐ Vinegar	☐ Plastic wrap or ziplock bags
☐ Soap	☐ Salt	☐ Sugar
☐ Chicken stock	☐ Anything else you can think of!	

HELPFUL HINTS

- To best measure your success, leave one cup of chicken stock with nothing added. You can compare it your other cups to see if what you add makes more or less bacteria or mold grow.
- Holding cups up to a light source will make it easier to compare cloudiness (an increase in cloudiness over time means an increase in bacteria or mold).
- Have an adult dispose of the sealed chicken stock samples in the garbage when you are done with the experiment. Always wash your hands after handling the cups.
- Add the same amount of ingredients each time.
- Try to add only clear ingredients so the liquids don't interfere with the cloudiness.
- Seal your cups with plastic wrap and tape (or pour your liquid into a ziplock bag that is sealed).
- Be sure to keep this experiment out of the reach of small children.

Real-life application

TAKE A LOOK AT THE INGREDIENTS IN SOME NATURAL CLEANERS (EITHER IN A STORE OR ONLINE). DO YOU SEE ANY INGREDIENTS YOU USED? DOES THIS GIVE YOU MORE IDEAS TO TRY?

Extensions

CAN YOU THINK OF THINGS YOU COULD ADD TO MAKE BACTERIA OR MOLD GROW FASTER?

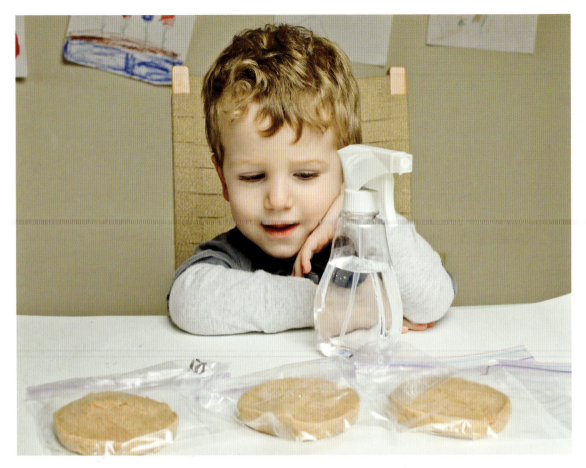

EXPERIMENT: DOES MOISTURE CHANGE HOW FAST FOOD MOLDS?

Will more water make it easier or harder for mold to grow? Or does moisture (water) not make a difference in mold growth?

MAKE YOUR GUESS: Do you think moisture will change how long it takes a food to mold?

THINGS TO CONSIDER WHEN RUNNING YOUR EXPERIMENT

Remember that the only thing you are changing is the amount of moisture (water) added. All other things should stay the same!

- What kind of food will you use for your experiment?
- Will you try different amounts of water? How much each time?
- How will you store your food so the water doesn't evaporate?
- Keep this experiment out of the reach of small children.

DATA

- How will you measure mold?
- How often will you check?

WHAT DID YOU LEARN FROM YOUR EXPERIMENT? WHAT HAPPENED? WHY DO YOU THINK IT HAPPENED?

Real-life application

WHY DO YOU THINK FOOD IS OFTEN STORED IN AIRTIGHT BAGS?

MARSHALL, AGE 4, ADDED BREAD TO ZIPLOCK BAGS. IN ONE BAG HE ADDED NO WATER, IN ANOTHER HE ADDED 2 SPRAYS OF WATER FROM A WATER BOTTLE, IN ANOTHER HE ADDED 3 SPRAYS OF WATER FROM A WATER BOTTLE, AND IN THE LAST BAG HE ADDED 4 SPRAYS OF WATER FROM A WATER BOTTLE. HE DECIDED TO HANG ALL THE BAGS FROM HIS CEILING. HE FOUND THAT THE BREAD IN THE BAG WITH NO WATER MOLDED FIRST.

ADVANCED LEVEL: What other questions do you have about moisture and mold? Design an experiment to answer a question.

EXPERIMENT: HOW WELL DO YOU WASH YOUR HANDS?

Though our skin is naturally covered with bacteria, we can pick up harmful bacteria, mold, and viruses during the day. Washing your hands with soap and water is a great way to wash off those unwanted germs, but do you wash your hands long enough and well enough to get them clean?

MAKE YOUR GUESS: Do you think you wash your hands well enough to remove most of the bacteria and mold?

THINGS TO CONSIDER WHEN RUNNING YOUR EXPERIMENT

Remember that the only thing you are changing is how long you wash your hands. All other things should stay the same!

- Be sure to touch lots of (the same) surfaces in between each hand washing to pick up more bacteria.
- How many different lengths of hand washing will you try? How many agar plates will you need to prepare? (See page 82 for how to make agar plates.)
- Hint: It's easiest to measure how much change the hand washing is having if you take a sample of unwashed hands to compare it to.

- Be sure to seal the edges of your plates with tape once you've swabbed them.
- Be sure to keep this experiment out of the reach of small children.

DATA

- How will you measure the amount of bacteria on each plate?
- How often will you check?

WHAT DID YOU LEARN FROM YOUR EXPERIMENT? WHAT HAPPENED? WHY DO YOU THINK IT HAPPENED?

Real-life application

WILL YOU WASH YOUR HANDS FOR A DIFFERENT AMOUNT OF TIME NOW?

DOCTORS AND NURSES OFTEN USE SPECIAL SCRUB BRUSHES TO WASH THEIR HANDS BEFORE SEEING PATIENTS WHO ARE VERY ILL. WHAT EFFECT DO YOU THINK USING SCRUB BRUSHES MIGHT HAVE ON THE AMOUNT OF BACTERIA LEFT BEHIND?

SAMANTHA, AGE 5, FOUND THAT SHE DID NOT WASH HER HANDS FOR LONG ENOUGH TO GET BACTERIA OFF. SHE CHOSE TO TRY TOUCHING THE BOTTOM OF HER SHOES IN BETWEEN EACH SAMPLE. FOR ONE SAMPLE SHE DIDN'T WASH AT ALL (0 SECONDS), FOR ANOTHER SHE WASHED ONLY FOR 1 SECOND, AND FOR THE LAST SAMPLE, SHE WASHED FOR 3 SECONDS. THE AGAR PLATES WITH SAMPLES FROM HER WASHED HANDS HAD SLIGHTLY FEWER BACTERIA THAN THE PLATE FROM HER UNWASHED HANDS. THERE WERE STILL A LOT OF BACTERIA AND MOLDS ON HER HANDS EVEN AFTER WASHING!

ADVANCED LEVEL: What other questions do you have about hand washing and bacteria? Design an experiment to answer a question.

EXPERIMENT: DOES TEMPERATURE CHANGE HOW FAST FOOD MOLDS?

Have you seen food mold before? What kinds of food? Pick a kind of food from your kitchen and design an experiment to see how different temperatures (cold, warm, hot) change how long it takes the food to grow mold.

MAKE YOUR GUESS: Do you think molds grow differently in different temperatures?

THINGS TO CONSIDER WHEN RUNNING YOUR EXPERIMENT

Remember that the only thing you are changing is the temperature. All other things should stay the same!

- What food will you use?
- How will you store it?
- Where will you find different temperatures? How many will you try?
- Keep this experiment out of the reach of small children.
- For safety, I recommend sealing your experiment so the mold isn't exposed to the air in your home or classroom.

DATA

- How will you measure mold growth?
- How often will you check?

WHAT DID YOU LEARN FROM YOUR EXPERIMENT? WHAT HAPPENED? WHY DO YOU THINK IT HAPPENED?

Real-life application

WHY DO YOU THINK WE FREEZE AND REFRIGERATE MANY KINDS OF FOOD?

DAISY, AGE 7, WANTED TO TEST FRUIT BECAUSE SHE "KNOWS IT MOLDS FAST." SHE CHOSE FOUR DIFFERENT PLACES TO PUT A RASPBERRY: OUTSIDE (COLD), INSIDE (WARM), ON A HEATER VENT (VERY WARM), AND IN THE FREEZER (VERY COLD). THE BERRY ON THE HEATER SHRIVELED RIGHT AWAY, BUT EVENTUALLY GREW A LITTLE MOLD. THE BERRY INSIDE GREW THE MOST MOLD. ON THE SECOND DAY, AN ANIMAL ATE THE OUTSIDE BERRY! THE RASPBERRY IN THE FREEZER NEVER MOLDED.

EXPLORE: ACTIVATING YEAST

Mix small amounts of yeast with a variety of water temperatures. What happens? How are they different? Try adding sugar to a few. What happens? Try adding salt to others. What happens?

MATERIALS

- [ ] Dry active yeast
- [ ] Salt
- [ ] Cups
- [ ] Sugar
- [ ] Water at various temperatures

HELPFUL HINTS

- Be sure to include one water temperature that is in the ideal range (indicated on the back of the yeast packet).
- Leave your yeast for at least 20 minutes to see the full effect.

Extensions

BAKE BREAD USING YEAST! MIX 2 CUPS OF ALL-PURPOSE FLOUR, 2 1/2 TEASPOONS OF YEAST, AND A SPRINKLE OF SALT IN A BOWL. IN ANOTHER BOWL HAVE AN ADULT HEAT 1 1/4 CUPS OF WATER TO THE TEMPERATURE NOTED ON YOUR YEAST PACKET. ADD 2 TABLESPOONS OF OLIVE OIL AND 1 TABLESPOON OF HONEY TO THE HEATED WATER AND STIR. HAVE AN ADULT POUR THE HEATED WATER INTO THE BOWL WITH THE FLOUR AND YEAST. MIX WELL, ADDING FLOUR BY THE TABLESPOON IF THE DOUGH IS VERY STICKY. ONCE YOU HAVE A SMOOTH DOUGH, COVER IT WITH A WARM, DAMP TOWEL, AND LEAVE IT FOR AN HOUR TO RISE. AFTER AN HOUR YOU SHOULD HAVE A VERY PUFFY DOUGH IF THE YEAST HAS DONE ITS JOB! ADD YOUR DOUGH TO AN OILED BREAD PAN AND COOK IT FOR 15 TO 20 MINUTES AT 400 DEGREES FAHRENHEIT OR UNTIL IT'S GOLDEN BROWN. ALLOW IT TO COOL (AND HAVE AN ADULT CHECK THE TEMPERATURE) BEFORE EATING.

EXPERIMENT: WHAT DOES YEAST EAT THE FASTEST?

Yeast gives off gas (carbon dioxide) when it eats. Can you find some foods in your kitchen that yeast will eat? Can you think of a fun way to catch the gas it might make?

MAKE YOUR GUESS: What type of food do you think yeast will eat the fastest?

THINGS TO CONSIDER WHEN RUNNING YOUR EXPERIMENT

Remember that the only thing you are changing is the type of food. All other things should stay the same!

- Read the instructions on your yeast packet to see how the brand recommends activating it. A general rule of thumb is to use ¼ cup of very warm water per packet of dry active yeast. You will add the entire activated mixture to either your ziplock bag or balloon.
- Yeast will give off carbon dioxide gas as it eats. If you seal your experiment in something, such as a ziplock bag or balloon, it will capture the gas.
- Remember to use the same amount of each food and the same amount of yeast each time.
- How many different foods will you try? Which ones?

DATA

- How will you measure which food the yeast ate the most of?
- How often will you check?

WHAT DID YOU LEARN FROM YOUR EXPERIMENT? WHAT HAPPENED? WHY DO YOU THINK IT HAPPENED?

Real life application

HOW DO YOU THINK YEAST HELPS MAKE BREAD RISE?

SAMANTHA, AGE 5, TRIED 3 TABLESPOONS EACH OF MASHED BANANAS, RAISINS, BREAD, AND REFRIED BEANS IN BALLOONS. SHE FOUND THAT THE BALLOON WITH THE RAISINS STARTED INFLATING RIGHT AWAY. AFTER 20 MINUTES, THE RAISINS AND BANANAS WERE MOSTLY INFLATED, THE BREAD WAS SLIGHTLY INFLATED, AND THE REFRIED BEANS WERE BARELY INFLATED.

ADVANCED LEVEL: What other questions do you have about yeast and food? Design an experiment to answer a question.

EXPLORE: MAKE YOUR OWN AGAR RECIPE

Take a look at our agar recipe on page 82. What sorts of things would you like to add or change? Bacteria are found almost everywhere on Earth. There are many that are specialized to live in extreme environments, for example, really salty places or in very hot or cold temperatures. Cook up your own recipe for agar and see what grows!

MATERIALS

- [ ] Beef broth
- [ ] Sugar
- [ ] Agar powder
- [ ] Salt
- [ ] Petri dishes or cups
- [ ] Anything else you can think of!

HELPFUL HINTS

- Make sure you add enough agar powder for the agar to be firm once it's cooled.
- Be sure to seal the edges of your petri dishes with tape once you've swabbed them.
- Keep this experiment out of the reach of small children.

EXPERIMENT: WHAT TEMPERATURE SHOULD WATER BE TO MAKE THE MOST ACTIVE YEAST?

Active dry yeast is cooking yeast that is "sleeping." By keeping it "asleep," the yeast stays usable for cooking for a long time. If you want to use yeast in a recipe, add water to "wake it up." "Awake" yeast will eat sugar and give off gas, and this gas is what makes baked goods rise and become fluffy. Can you figure out what temperature of water will wake up the most of your sleeping yeast?

MAKE YOUR GUESS: Which temperature of water do you think will wake up the most active dry yeast?

THINGS TO CONSIDER WHEN RUNNING YOUR EXPERIMENT

Remember that the only thing you are changing is the temperature of the water you are adding to the yeast. All other things should stay the same!

- How many different water temperatures will you test?
- How will you capture the gas to measure how awake your yeast are?
- How much sugar will you add to each water temperature?
- How much yeast will you add to each water temperature?

DATA

- How will you decide if the yeast are awake?
- Will you measure anything?
- How often will you check? (Hint: Yeast usually takes 20 to 40 minutes to fully wake up.)

HELPFUL HINTS

- If you want to try very warm, hot, or boiling water, please have an adult help handle and prepare it.
- Ziplock bags, balloons, and other plastic containers may not hold up to high heat. If you'd like to use a ziplock bag, place a microwave-safe cup inside the bag to hold the heated water and seal the ziplock bag around the cup.
- Because the yeast reaction takes some time to get started, it's fine to take a little time to be sure the container is completely sealed.
- Be sure to mix the yeast, sugar, and water well.

WHAT DID YOU LEARN FROM YOUR EXPERIMENT? WHAT HAPPENED? WHY DO YOU THINK IT HAPPENED?

Real-life application

CHECK THE BACK OF YOUR ACTIVE DRY YEAST PACKET OR BOTTLE. WHAT TEMPERATURE DOES IT RECOMMEND FOR ACTIVATING YEAST? DID YOU FIND THE SAME THING IN YOUR EXPERIMENT? WHAT DO YOU THINK BREAD COOKED WITH YEAST MIXED IN COLD WATER WOULD LOOK LIKE? THERE IS A BREAD RECIPE ON PAGE 102 IF YOU WANT TO TEST IT OUT!

SAMANTHA, AGE 5, CHOSE TO TRY FOUR DIFFERENT WATER TEMPERATURES: 40 DEGREES FAHRENHEIT, 68 DEGREES FAHRENHEIT, 82 DEGREES FAHRENHEIT, AND 120 DEGREES FAHRENHEIT (WITH ADULT HELP). SHE ADDED 1 DROP OF PINK FOOD COLORING, 3 SUGAR CUBES, AND 1 TABLESPOON OF DRY ACTIVE YEAST TO EACH OF THE FOUR CUPS OF WATER, STIRRED EACH WELL, AND HAD AN ADULT PLACE THEM IN A ZIPLOCK BAG AND SEAL THEM. AFTER 40 MINUTES, THE BAG WITH 120 DEGREE WATER POPPED! THE 82 DEGREE WATER BAG WAS VERY FULL OF GAS, AND THE 68 DEGREE WATER BAG WAS SLIGHTLY FULL OF GAS. SAMANTHA WAS PRETTY SURE THAT THE 40 DEGREE WATER BAG DID NOT MAKE ANY GAS.

ADVANCED LEVEL: What other questions do you have about yeast and temperature? Design an experiment to answer a question.

Chapter 4
Engineering

INTRODUCTION

Engineering is all about building and creating. It requires a lot of problem solving. Successful engineering projects require lots of attempts. Each time you do an experiment, you can look at what worked and what didn't, and keep trying new solutions for the parts that aren't working. The engineering activities in this chapter are meant to be tried many times. Each time you'll find yourself learning more about what makes something successful. Have fun and don't give up!

> **"If at first you don't succeed, try, try, try again."**
> –WILLIAM EDWARD HICKSON

SUPPLY LIST FOR THE ACTIVITIES IN THE ENGINEERING CHAPTER

- [ ] Hard-boiled eggs
- [ ] Cups
- [ ] Tape
- [ ] Cotton balls
- [ ] Paper towels
- [ ] Styrofoam (optional)
- [ ] Wooden craft sticks (Popsicle sticks)

- [ ] Foil
- [ ] Pennies
- [ ] Bubble mix (store-bought or use your own from page 70)
- [ ] Straws
- [ ] Paper
- [ ] Scissors
- [ ] Yarn or string
- [ ] Rubber bands
- [ ] Plastic spoon
- [ ] Clean items from your recycling bin
- [ ] Marble (or other small ball)
- [ ] Pom poms
- [ ] Paper clips
- [ ] Matchbox cars
- [ ] Ramps (wood scraps from a hardware store, cardboard from your recycling bin, or plastic such as rain gutter scraps from a hardware store)
- [ ] Tape measure or ruler
- [ ] Balloons

EXPLORE: DESIGN A RAMP TO MAKE CARS ROLL FARTHER

Using a toy car and a ramp made of wood or cardboard, try different heights by propping it on different sized books or boxes. Mark how far your car rolls each time. Is steeper always better? Is there a perfect ramp height for making your car roll the farthest?

MATERIALS

- ☐ Books or boxes
- ☐ Car
- ☐ Ramp made of cardboard or wood
- ☐ Something to mark distances (for example, sticky notes or pennies)

HELPFUL HINTS

- Use a wide ramp to make it easier to keep the car on it, or design bumpers for the edges!
- Use the same ramp and car each time.
- If you use a wood ramp, have an adult check it for splinters or sharp edges.

Extensions

DOES THE BEST RAMP HEIGHT CHANGE IF YOU CHANGE THE SURFACE? TRY YOUR RAMP EXPERIMENT ON DIFFERENT SURFACES (FOR EXAMPLE, CARPET, GRAVEL, CEMENT, WOOD FLOORS).

CHALLENGE: DESIGN AN EGG DROP CONTAINER

Can you design a package that keeps the egg's shell from cracking when you drop it?

MISSION: Keep the hard-boiled egg's shell from cracking.

MATERIALS

- ☐ Hard-boiled egg
- ☐ Cup or box
- ☐ Tape
- ☐ Rubber bands
- ☐ Towels
- ☐ Styrofoam
- ☐ Cotton balls
- ☐ Paper
- ☐ Paper towels
- ☐ Pom poms
- ☐ Tissue paper
- ☐ Wooden craft sticks
- ☐ String
- ☐ Plastic wrap
- ☐ Foil
- ☐ And anything else you can think of!

HELPFUL HINTS

- Try as many different ideas as you can think of!
- Be sure to have an adult boil the eggs first if you don't want a big mess.

Real-life application

THE NEXT TIME YOU GET A PACKAGE IN THE MAIL, LOOK AT HOW IT WAS PACKAGED (ALTERNATIVELY, TAKE A TRIP TO THE POST OFFICE AND SEE WHAT SUPPLIES ARE AVAILABLE OR WATCH PEOPLE PACKAGE BOXES). DO YOU SEE ANY SIMILARITIES BETWEEN THIS AND WHAT YOU TRIED? DOES IT GIVE YOU MORE IDEAS?

Extensions

TRY GOING HIGHER AND HIGHER WITH YOUR BEST DESIGNS. IF YOU DON'T HAVE A TWO-STORY HOUSE, PLAYGROUNDS WORK WELL TO SAFELY GET UP HIGH.

TRY A SMALLER CONTAINER OR BOX. IS IT EASIER OR HARDER TO KEEP THE EGG'S SHELL FROM CRACKING?

CHALLENGE: BUILD A FOIL BOAT THAT WILL HOLD THE MOST WEIGHT

Which boat design will hold the most weight before sinking?

MISSION: Design a foil boat that can hold the most weight before sinking.

MATERIALS

- ☐ Foil
- ☐ Weights (pennies, paper clips, or beads)
- ☐ Bathtub or container filled with water.

HELPFUL HINTS

- Try several different shapes.
- Use the same sized piece of foil each time.
- Experiment with how and where (stacking or spreading out, middle or sides) you place the weights to see if that has an effect.

Extensions

TRY USING MORE FOIL. DOES A BIGGER BOAT HOLD MORE WEIGHT?

TRY ADDING ANOTHER ITEM TO YOUR BOAT-BUILDING SUPPLIES, SUCH AS WOODEN CRAFT STICKS. HOW DOES THIS CHANGE THE NUMBER OF WEIGHTS (PENNIES, PAPER CLIPS, OR BEADS) YOU ARE ABLE TO ADD?

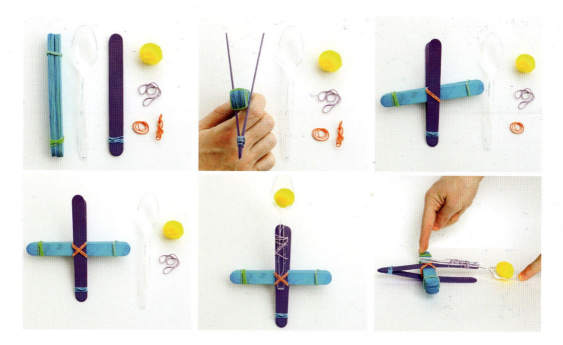

EXPLORE: CHANGE A CATAPULT TO SEE HOW FAR IT CAN TOSS AN ITEM

Create a simple catapult using the directions below. Measure how far it tosses a light, soft item (for example, a pom pom or marshmallow). Now begin changing elements of the catapult (for example, the tightness of the rubber bands, the length of the spoon) and observe how these modifications change how far the catapult can toss your item.

MATERIALS

☐ Rubber bands

☐ Pom pom or marshmallow

☐ Wooden craft sticks

☐ Spoon

DIRECTIONS

1. Gather several wooden craft sticks in a stacked pile and secure each end with rubber bands.

2. Lay two sticks on top of each other and secure one end with a rubber band.

3. Pull the two sticks slightly apart (making a "v") and place the large rubber banded pile in the center to keep the sticks pulled apart.

4. Use a rubber band to secure the upper stick to the stacked pile of sticks.

5. Use a rubber band to secure a plastic spoon to the upper stick.

6. Place a pom pom or marshmallow in the spoon.

7. Hold the catapult steady with one hand while pulling the spoon with the pom pom or marshmallow toward the ground with the other hand.

8. Let the spoon go and watch the pom pom or marshmallow fly!

HELPFUL HINTS

- Mark the distance your item is thrown with sticky notes or pennies or some other kind of marker.

Extensions

CAN YOU DESIGN A CATAPULT THAT WILL TOSS YOUR ITEM ONLY A VERY SHORT DISTANCE? WHAT ABOUT A CATAPULT THAT TOSSES THINGS VERY HIGH?

CAN YOU DESIGN A COMPLETELY DIFFERENT CATAPULT? GIVE IT A TRY.

CHALLENGE: DESIGN A BUBBLE BLOWER

Can you transform an ordinary plastic cup into a cool bubble blower?

MISSION: Transform a plastic cup into a bubble blower.

MATERIALS

- [ ] Plastic cup
- [ ] Balloon
- [ ] Bubble solution (or make your own using the activity on page 72)
- [ ] Anything else you can think of!
- [ ] Tape
- [ ] Straws
- [ ] Scissors
- [ ] Plastic wrap
- [ ] Foil

HELPFUL HINTS

- Adults are very good at cutting cups.
- If you cut a plastic cup, watch for sharp edges.
- Remember to always blow out and never suck in bubble solution.

Extensions

CAN YOU CREATE A BUBBLE BLOWER THAT MAKES LARGER BUBBLES? WHAT ABOUT A BUBBLE BLOWER THAT MAKES SMALLER BUBBLES? WHAT ABOUT A BUBBLE BLOWER THAT BLOWS SEVERAL BUBBLES AT ONCE?

CHALLENGE: DESIGN A BRIDGE
THAT WILL HOLD THE MOST WEIGHT

Can you design a strong bridge out of paper and tape?

MISSION: Using paper and tape, can you create a bridge that holds the most weight?

MATERIALS

☐ Paper ☐ Tape ☐ Scissors ☐ Weights (for example, pennies or gems)

HELPFUL HINTS

- Folded paper is stronger than flat paper.
- Try several different designs.
- Use the same amount of paper for each bridge design.

Real-life application

LOOK AT PHOTOS OF BRIDGES ON THE COMPUTER OR TRAVEL TO A NEARBY BRIDGE. DO YOU SEE SIMILARITIES BETWEEN THE REAL-LIFE BRIDGES AND YOUR DESIGNS? DO THE REAL-LIFE EXAMPLES GIVE YOU MORE IDEAS TO TRY?

Extensions

ADD ANOTHER MATERIAL OF YOUR CHOICE TO YOUR BRIDGE-BUILDING SUPPLIES. DOES ADDING THIS SUPPLY MAKE YOUR BRIDGE STRONGER? WHY OR WHY NOT?

EXPLORE: CHANGE A BALLOON ROCKET TO MAKE IT GO FARTHER

Using the longest distance inside your home (or outside), set up a balloon rocket track by stringing several feet of yarn or string between two level objects (for example, two chairs). Tape a straw to your balloons and thread them onto the track by running the yarn through the straw. Blow up the balloon (or have an adult blow it up) and let it go. Mark the distance it travels. Now add things to your balloon (for example, wings, fins, a nose, or anything you can think of!). How do your additions change the distance the balloon rocket travels?

MATERIALS

- ☐ Balloons
- ☐ Yarn or string
- ☐ Tape
- ☐ Paper
- ☐ Straw
- ☐ Two chairs
- ☐ Scissors

HELPFUL HINTS

- It is easier to add things to the balloon once it's inflated.

Extensions

TRY DIFFERENTLY SHAPED BALLOONS AND SEE HOW THE SHAPE CHANGES THE DISTANCE TRAVELED.

CAN YOU DESIGN A BALLOON THAT TRAVELS ONLY A VERY SHORT DISTANCE?

CHALLENGE: DESIGN A TALL TOWER OUT OF STRAWS AND TAPE

Can you design a super tall tower out of just straws and tape? Do you think you can build a tower that is taller than yourself? How about a tower taller than your parents?

MISSION: Build a super tall tower out of straws and tape.

MATERIALS: Straws and tape.

HELPFUL HINTS

- If you get stuck, think of the shape of tall buildings.
- If your structure is tipping over, make a wider base.

Extensions

PUT TWO CHAIRS ABOUT 4 FEET APART. TRY TO BUILD A BRIDGE OF STRAWS AND TAPE BETWEEN THE TWO CHAIRS. ONCE YOU'VE ACCOMPLISHED THAT, TRY A LARGER DISTANCE BETWEEN THE TWO CHAIRS.

CHALLENGE: DESIGN A MARBLE RUN FROM YOUR RECYCLING BIN

Can you design a working marble run using recycled items from your house?

MISSION: Collect clean recycled materials for a week or so and use them to design a working marble run.

MATERIALS

- [ ] Any recycled materials
- [ ] Painter's tape
- [ ] Scissors
- [ ] Can opener (with adult help)
- [ ] Marbles
- [ ] Large piece of cardboard (optional)

HELPFUL HINTS

- Painter's tape is less likely to damage a wall than regular tape. If you are worried about taping materials to your wall, use a large piece of cardboard instead.

- If you are using cans, have an adult inspect them for any sharp edges. If you need to use a can opener, have an adult do it for you.

- If you need any plastic containers cut, you may want to ask an adult for help. Also check any cut plastic for sharp edges.

- Using painter's tape should allow you to readjust the items you are placing in your marble run.

Extensions

TRY SOMETHING LIGHTER THAN MARBLES, SUCH AS POM POMS. DOES YOUR MARBLE RUN STILL WORK OR DO YOU NEED TO ADJUST SOME OF THE ITEMS?

MAKE A MARBLE RUN WITH THREE OR MORE TURNS IN IT.

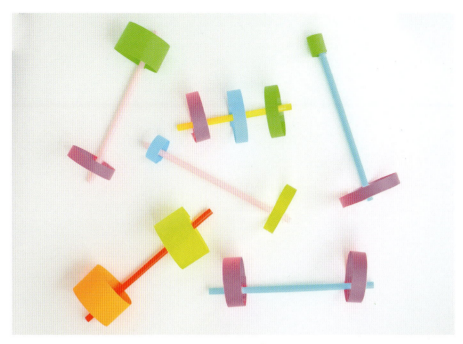

EXPLORE: DESIGN A STRAW PLANE AND CHANGE THE PARTS TO CHANGE HOW IT FLIES

How do the different elements (for example, the length of straw, number of paper circles, width of paper circles, size of paper circles) of a basic straw plane change how the plane flies? Use the directions below to make a basic straw plane and work from there!

MATERIALS

☐ Paper ☐ Straws ☐ Scissors ☐ Tape

HELPFUL HINT

- Remember if you change just one thing at a time, it's easier to tell what that change does.

Extensions

HOW ARE AIRPLANES SHAPED? DID YOU TRY THIS SHAPE WITH YOUR PLANE? HOW DID IT FLY?

USE A TAPE MEASURE TO MEASURE HOW FAR YOUR LONGEST-FLYING PLANE CAN FLY.

CAN YOU DESIGN A PLANE THAT CAN FLY IN A LOOP?

DESIGN A PLANE WITH JUST PAPER, TAPE, AND STRAWS THAT HAS NO PAPER CIRCLES ON IT. DOES IT FLY AS FAR? WHY DO YOU THINK THIS IS?

EXPERIMENT: HOW DOES WEIGHT CHANGE HOW FAR A CAR WILL ROLL?

Do heavier things roll farther? Find out if adding weight to a toy car will make it roll a longer or shorter distance.

MAKE YOUR GUESS: How do you think adding weight to a car will change the distance it rolls?

THINGS TO CONSIDER WHEN RUNNING YOUR EXPERIMENT

Remember that the only thing you are changing is the amount of weight added to the car. All other things should stay the same!

- How will you add weight?
- How many different amounts of your weight will you test?

DATA

- How will you measure the distance the car will roll?
- How will you measure the weight you're adding each time?

WHAT DID YOU LEARN FROM YOUR EXPERIMENT? WHAT HAPPENED? WHY DO YOU THINK IT HAPPENED?

Real–life application

HOW HEAVY DO YOU THINK YOUR FAMILY CAR IS? WHY DO YOU THINK YOUR PARENTS NEED TO KEEP A BIG SPACE BETWEEN YOUR CAR AND THE CAR IN FRONT OF YOU ON THE FREEWAY?

HENRI, AGE 4, CHOSE TO ADD LARGE GEMS TO A CAR WITH TAPE. HE MARKED THE DISTANCE THE CARS TRAVELED ON THE CARPET WITH WOODEN CRAFT STICKS. HE FOUND THAT ADDING MORE WEIGHT MADE HIS CAR TRAVEL FARTHER.

ADVANCED LEVEL: What other questions do you have about cars and weights? Design an experiment to answer a question.

EXPERIMENT: WHAT CONTAINER SHAPE WILL PRODUCE THE TALLEST BUBBLE TOWER?

If you fill a container with a small amount of bubble solution (or dish soap mixed with water), place a straw in the bubbles, and blow—you will create a tower built of bubbles! After it reaches a certain height, your bubble tower will tip over. Does the shape of the container you are blowing bubbles in change how high your bubble tower will grow before tipping over?

MAKE YOUR GUESS: Which container shape will produce the tallest tower of bubbles?

THINGS TO CONSIDER WHEN RUNNING YOUR EXPERIMENT

Remember that the only thing you are changing is the shape of the container you are using. All other things should stay the same!

- How many different container shapes will you try?
- How much bubble solution will you put in each container?

DATA

- How will you decide which tower is the tallest?
- Will you measure anything?

HELPFUL HINTS

- If you'd like to mix your own bubble solution, you can do so by adding a few teaspoons of dish soap per cup of water and stirring gently until it is well mixed. Alternatively, you could complete the challenge on page 72 first and use the recipe you develop.
- Have an adult take a pair of scissors and cut a small diamond-shaped notch out of the straw about 2 inches from the top. This will prevent accidental inhalation of the bubble solution, but will still allow you to blow a bubble tower.
- Please wear goggles to protect eyes from soapy water.

WHAT DID YOU LEARN FROM YOUR EXPERIMENT? WHAT HAPPENED? WHY DO YOU THINK IT HAPPENED?

SAMANTHA, AGE 5, CHOSE TO TRY FIVE DIFFERENT CONTAINERS. SHE WAS SURPRISED TO FIND THAT THE LONG RECTANGULAR PAN SUPPORTED THE TALLEST BUBBLE TOWER.

ADVANCED LEVEL: What other questions do you have about bubble towers and container shapes? Design an experiment to answer a question.

CHALLENGE: DESIGN A BALLOON-POWERED CAR

Can you create a car that is powered by the air rushing out of a balloon?

MISSION: Create a car that moves when you release the air from an attached blown-up balloon.

MATERIALS

☐ Balloon

☐ Tape

- ☐ Straws
- ☐ Cardstock
- ☐ Paper towel tubes
- ☐ Other materials from your recycling bin

HELPFUL HINTS

- It is easiest to try your car on a smooth surface, such as a wood or linoleum floor (like a kitchen or bathroom floor).
- You may need adult help to blow up the balloon each time.

Extensions

CAN YOU DESIGN A FLOATING BOAT THAT IS POWERED BY BALLOON?

DOES YOUR CAR TRAVEL DIFFERENT DISTANCES ON DIFFERENT SURFACES (FOR EXAMPLE, GRASS, CARPET, ETC)? WHY DO YOU THINK THIS IS?

CAN YOU DESIGN A LIGHTWEIGHT PLANE THAT WILL FLY THROUGH THE AIR USING BALLOON POWER?

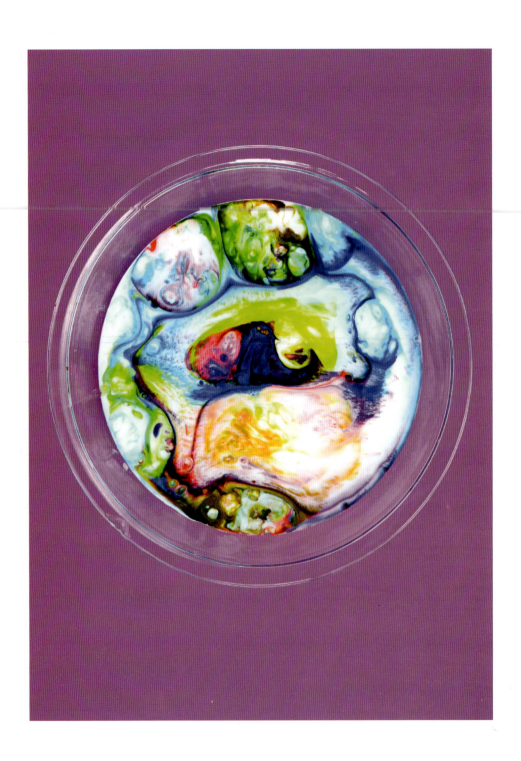

Chapter 5
Food and Candy

INTRODUCTION

Did you know that the food in your kitchen can be used to demonstrate several different scientific concepts? In this chapter we'll cover a variety of topics as we investigate food and candy.

RED CABBAGE JUICE RECIPE

For some of the experiments, you'll need to prepare red cabbage juice. Red cabbage juice is used as a pH indicator. Every material has a certain color it turns when added to red cabbage juice. For instance, baking soda always turns blue when added to red cabbage juice. In this book, we'll use red cabbage juice to give us a hint about what a mystery substance is. We'll also have fun finding out what color something turns when added to red cabbage juice. To make red cabbage juice for the activities on page 157, 158, and 159, you'll need:

☐ Red cabbage

☐ Water

☐ Blender

Add four or five red cabbage leaves per 1 cup of water to a blender and blend until the red cabbage turns to liquid. You can use it as is (some of the cabbage bits will settle out of the mixture, but this won't interfere with its ability to change color when something is added) or you can use a coffee filter to filter out the remaining cabbage bits and leave just the purple liquid behind.

SUPPLY LIST FOR THE ACTIVITIES IN THIS CHAPTER

- [ ] M&M's
- [ ] Oil
- [ ] Vinegar
- [ ] Salt
- [ ] Ziplock bags
- [ ] Plastic cups
- [ ] Sugar
- [ ] Lemon juice
- [ ] Paper towels
- [ ] Flour
- [ ] Cornstarch
- [ ] Baking soda
- [ ] Baking powder
- [ ] Epsom salt
- [ ] Alum (found in the spice section of most grocery stores; our favorite brand for producing large alum crystals is Kroger)
- [ ] Pipe cleaners (chenille stems from a craft store)
- [ ] String
- [ ] Paper
- [ ] Coffee filters
- [ ] Markers (the pack from the Dollar Tree is our favorite)
- [ ] Different types of milk (for example, 2%, whole, skim, half-and-half, almond, soy)
- [ ] Cotton swabs (such as Q-tips)
- [ ] Sugar cubes
- [ ] Candy color
- [ ] Gummy bears or worms
- [ ] Dish soap
- [ ] Juice or soda
- [ ] Eggs
- [ ] Food coloring
- [ ] Corn syrup
- [ ] Red cabbage

EXPERIMENT: WHAT LIQUID GETS THE "M" OFF AN M&M THE FASTEST?

As you dissolve the colored candy coating off an M&M, the "M" will usually stay in one piece. And because it's made out of wax, it's less dense (there's less "stuff" in the same space) than water and will float! It can be a little tricky to get it off in one piece, but it's possible!

MAKE YOUR GUESS: What liquid do you think will get the "M" off an M&M the fastest?

THINGS TO CONSIDER WHEN RUNNING YOUR EXPERIMENT

Remember that the only thing you are changing is the type of liquid. All other things should stay the same!

- How many different liquids will you try?
- How much of each liquid?
- Will you try different temperatures of different liquids? (Have an adult prepare, test, and supervise any heated liquids)
- If you stir, it will probably destroy the "M." Let the M&M sit undisturbed in the liquid to give you the best shot at getting a whole "M" to float to the surface.

- How will you measure how quickly the "M" comes off?

WHAT DID YOU LEARN FROM YOUR EXPERIMENT? WHAT HAPPENED? WHY DO YOU THINK IT HAPPENED?

HENRI, AGE 4, CHOSE TO TRY HOT WATER AND ICY COLD WATER. HE WAS SURPRISED TO FIND THAT THE HOT WATER REMOVED THE "M" MUCH MORE QUICKLY THAN THE ICY COLD WATER.

ADVANCED LEVEL: What other questions do you have about liquids and M&Ms? Design an experiment to answer a question.

CHALLENGE: KEEP APPLE SLICES FROM TURNING BROWN

Have you ever noticed that apple slices turn brown if they are left out? Can you design a solution to keep them from turning brown?

MISSION: Keep cut apple slices from turning brown.

MATERIALS

- [ ] Ziplock bags
- [ ] Salt
- [ ] Lemon juice
- [ ] Vinegar
- [ ] Sugar
- [ ] Paper towels
- [ ] Water
- [ ] Cooking oil
- [ ] Anything else you can think of!

HELPFUL HINTS

- Try to use the same sized apple slice each time.

Real-life application

THE INSIDE OF AN APPLE WILL TURN BROWN BECAUSE OF A CHEMICAL REACTION BETWEEN AIR AND THE FRUIT. CAN YOU THINK OF OTHER FRUITS THAT DO THE SAME THING?

BAGS OF APPLE SLICES AT THE GROCERY STORE ARE NEVER BROWN. TAKE A TRIP TO YOUR LOCAL STORE AND CHECK OUT THE INGREDIENTS ON THE BAG. CAN YOU FIGURE OUT HOW THEY KEEP FROM TURNING BROWN? DID YOU TRY THIS IN YOUR EXPERIMENT?

EXPLORE: MAKE GUMMY WORMS (OR BEARS) GROW AND SHRINK

Can you add kitchen ingredients to change the size of gummy worms or bears overnight?

MATERIALS

- ☐ Smooth gummy bears or worms
- ☐ Cups or ziplock bags
- ☐ Anything else you can think of!
- ☐ Salt
- ☐ Water
- ☐ Vinegar
- ☐ Sugar
- ☐ Juice
- ☐ Soda

HELPFUL HINTS

- Try rolling the gummy bears or worms in dry ingredients and soaking them in different solutions.
- Be sure to allow enough time for a change to take place!
- Do not eat your gummy bears or worms after testing.

Extensions

DO YOU THINK GUMMY BEARS OR WORMS WOULD DO THE SAME THING IF YOU CHANGED THE TEMPERATURE OF THE LIQUIDS YOU ADDED THEM TO? TRY IT AND FIND OUT.

CHALLENGE: MAKE AN EGG FLOAT
BY ADDING INGREDIENTS

If you place an egg in a cup full of water, it will sink. Can you add ingredients from your kitchen to the cup of water and make the egg float?

MISSION: Add ingredients from your kitchen to see if you can make an egg float.

MATERIALS

☐ Egg in a large cup with water added (enough to cover the top of the egg by a few inches)

☐ Various kitchen ingredients such as sugar, salt, oil, vinegar, carbonated water or soda

HELPFUL TIPS

- If you are adding a solid (like salt or sugar), make sure you stir to dissolve it. If you're having trouble getting your egg to float, try a new ingredient or try adding larger amounts of your ingredients (for example, increasing from ¼ to ½ cup or 1 to 2 teaspoons).

Real-life application

HAVE YOU EVER NOTICED THAT IT IS EASIER TO FLOAT IN THE OCEAN? THIS IS BECAUSE OCEAN WATER IS MORE DENSE THAN REGULAR WATER. DENSITY IS A MEASURE OF HOW MUCH STUFF THERE IS IN A SPACE. WHEN YOU ADD SALT TO WATER, THERE IS MORE STUFF IN THE SAME AMOUNT OF SPACE. IF SOMETHING IS LESS DENSE THAN SOMETHING ELSE, IT FLOATS. YOU ARE LESS DENSE THAN SALT WATER, SO YOU FLOAT!

137

EXPLORE: ADD "NAKED" EGGS TO DIFFERENT LIQUIDS

Prepare colored "naked" eggs according to the directions below. Place one egg in each cup and fill each cup with a different clear liquid. Leave the eggs for several hours or overnight in the refrigerator. What happens to your eggs? Why do you think this is?

MATERIALS

- [ ] Naked eggs (prepared according to directions below)
- [ ] Cups
- [ ] Different clear liquids (for example, vinegar, corn syrup, carbonated water, clear soda, salt water, sugar water, soapy water, and anything else you can think of!).

DIRECTIONS FOR PREPARING NAKED EGGS

1. Add one egg to a tall cup and add enough vinegar to cover the egg. Leave the egg for 24 hours in the refrigerator.

2. After 24 hours, drain the vinegar and rinse the egg, and add a new batch of vinegar and leave the eggs in the refrigerator for an additional 24 hours.

3. Have an adult gently rinse the eggs under running water to remove any remaining shell. You now have an egg with just the membrane, and no shell—a naked egg!

4. You can soak the naked egg in colored water overnight to add color to it before experimenting if you'd like.

HELPFUL HINTS

- If you use clear or nearly clear liquids, it will be easier to observe the changes in your eggs.
- Always wash your hands after handling eggs.

Extensions

TRY THIS EXPERIMENT WITH RAISINS. DO YOU GET THE SAME RESULTS? WHY DO YOU THINK THIS IS?

AFTER COMPLETING THE ACTIVITIES IN CHAPTER 6 (BAKING SODA AND VINEGAR), CAN YOU GUESS WHY YOU SEE BUBBLES ON THE EGG SHELLS WHEN YOU ADD VINEGAR? CAN YOU GUESS WHY YOU NEED TO ADD NEW VINEGAR THE NEXT DAY?

CHALLENGE: MAKE PLAY DOUGH

Squishy, stretchy, soft—dough is so fun to play with. Can you make play dough out of kitchen ingredients?

MISSION: Make play dough out of kitchen ingredients.

MATERIALS: Some combination of flour, cornstarch, salt, water, oatmeal, water, cooking oil, and baking soda.

HELPFUL HINTS

- If your dough is too dry, add more liquid. If it is too wet, add more dry ingredients.
- Unless you use a lot of salt, your dough is likely to mold after a day or two.

Extensions

WHAT HAPPENS IF YOU TRY TO AIR DRY YOUR DOUGH?

WHAT HAPPENS IF YOU BAKE IT AT A LOW TEMPERATURE?

IS YOUR DOUGH STRETCHY? IF NOT, CAN YOU MAKE A STRETCHY DOUGH?

EXPLORE: MAKE EPSOM SALT CRYSTALS

A crystal is what happens when a molecule (very tiny bit of something) makes a repeating pattern over and over when it forms a solid. The repeating pattern creates a solid that has cool edges and shapes. A snowflake is a crystal that is made when water (a liquid) freezes into a solid (ice) in a really cool pattern. You may have also seen rocks with crystals inside them. Did you know there are some kitchen ingredients you can use to make crystals? If you mix these special ingredients with water to make a liquid and allow them to evaporate (dry out), you'll grow crystals. Making crystals can be a bit tricky. If you don't mix in (dissolve) enough of the ingredient, there won't be enough stuff to grow a bunch of big, pretty crystals. See if you can create a mixture that makes big, beautiful Epsom salt crystals form!

MATERIALS

- [ ] Epsom salts
- [ ] Hot or cold or warm water
- [ ] Measuring spoons
- [ ] Shallow dishes
- [ ] Cups (glass if you are going to use boiling hot water)
- [ ] Cardboard pieces

HELPFUL HINTS

- Try adding different amounts of Epsom salts to different temperatures of water. Be sure to write down what you try.

- Once you've made your solutions (the mix of water and Epsom salt), leave them out to dry. If you have the right mix to make crystals, the crystals will form as the water evaporates. (Hint: Small amounts of water will evaporate the fastest. This process can take several days to a week, depending on how much water you used.)

- For faster results, dip cardboard pieces in each solution and allow them to dry. If you have a mix that will form crystals, a thin layer of crystals will appear on the cardboard after an hour or two.

- If you'd like to use boiling or very hot water, be sure to have an adult prepare and handle it.

EXPERIMENT: CAN YOU MIX TWO CRYSTALLIZING INGREDIENTS AND STILL GET CRYSTALS?

Do you need to have just one crystallizing ingredient dissolved in water to make crystals? Or can you mix two? Will you get a mix of the two crystals or an entirely new type of crystal?

MAKE YOUR GUESS: Do you think you will still get crystals if you mix Epsom salts and alum?

THINGS TO CONSIDER WHEN RUNNING YOUR EXPERIMENT

Remember that the only thing you are changing is mixing different combinations of alum and Epsom salts. All other things should stay the same!

- I recommend completing the activity on page 141 first to get a feel for how to make crystals.
- How many different combinations will you try? How much of each ingredient will you add?
- How much water will you use? How warm will it be? (Hint: less water means you will get results faster, since crystals form as water evaporates)
- How long will you run your experiment? (Hint: Epsom salt crystals can take up to two weeks to form)

DATA

- How will you decide if crystals have formed?

WHAT DID YOU LEARN FROM YOUR EXPERIMENT? WHAT HAPPENED? WHY DO YOU THINK IT HAPPENED?

ROSA, AGE 8, MIXED ONE CUP OF HOT WATER WITH EPSOM SALT AND ONE CUP OF HOT WATER WITH ALUM. THEN SHE MIXED SEVERAL CUPS WITH DIFFERENT AMOUNTS OF THE EPSOM SALT WATER AND ALUM WATER. SHE FOUND THAT ALL THE MIXTURES CRYSTALLIZED AFTER A FEW DAYS.

ADVANCED LEVEL: What other questions do you have about crystallizing ingredients and crystals? Design an experiment to answer a question.

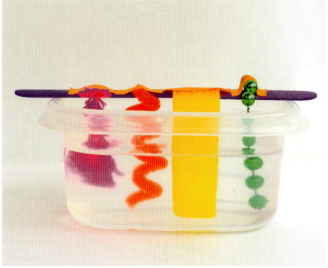

CHALLENGE: FIND THE BEST WAY
TO GROW ALUM CRYSTALS

Some crystal growing kits have you pour solution into a shallow container and add cardboard or rocks. Other crystal growing kits have you hang pipe cleaners, yarn, string, or sticks from the top of a cup of solution. Which method grows the most alum crystals?

MISSION: Test a variety of materials and methods to see which grow the most crystals.

MATERIALS

☐ Alum (from the spices section of your grocery store; our favorite brand for producing large alum crystals is Kroeger)

☐ Cups or beakers or dishes

☐ Water

☐ Various materials such as cardboard shapes, rocks, pipe cleaners, yarn, string, sticks, and anything else you can think of!

HELPFUL HINTS

- Crystals are grown from a super-saturated solution. To make a super-saturated solution, you'll need an adult to keep adding alum to boiling hot water and stirring until no more alum will dissolve.

- There is more than one type of alum. The kind that crystallizes is in the spices section of a grocery store. If you order it online, check the description or reviews to be sure you have the type that crystallizes (potassium aluminum sulfate). Please note that the full name will not always be listed, depending on the brand.

- Remember to start with the same amount of a super-saturated solution of alum each time.

- Alum typically takes 24 to 48 hours to finish crystallizing.

- To save on cost, you can hang several items in the same container of super-saturated alum at the same time.

- You can try pouring amounts of the solution in shallow dishes and adding rocks or cardboard or other items.

Extensions

DOES THE ANSWER CHANGE WHEN YOU USE A DIFFERENT CRYSTALLIZING INGREDIENT, SUCH AS EPSOM SALTS? (PLEASE NOTE THAT EPSOM SALT CRYSTALS MAY TAKE TWO WEEKS OR MORE TO FORM.)

EXPERIMENT: DOES TEMPERATURE CHANGE HOW QUICKLY FOOD COLORING SPREADS?

Do you think hot water will spread food coloring the most quickly? Or will icy cold water? Will they both do the same thing?

MAKE YOUR GUESS: Do you think different temperatures of water will change how quickly food coloring spreads?

THINGS TO CONSIDER WHEN RUNNING YOUR EXPERIMENT

Remember that the only thing you are changing is the temperature of your water. All other things should stay the same!

- How many different temperatures do you want to test? What are they?
- How many drops of food coloring will you add to each?
- If you are using very hot water, have an adult prepare and handle it.

DATA:

- How will you measure how long it takes the food coloring to spread completely through the water?

WHAT DID YOU LEARN FROM YOUR EXPERIMENT? WHAT HAPPENED? WHY DO YOU THINK IT HAPPENED?

Real-life application

MOLECULES ARE THE SMALLEST BITS OF THINGS—SO SMALL THAT YOU CAN'T SEE THEM. WHEN THEY ARE WARM, THEY MOVE FASTER! THE WATER MOLECULES AND FOOD COLORING MOLECULES IN THE HOT WATER MOVED FASTER THAN THE WATER MOLECULES AND FOOD COLORING MOLECULES IN THE COLD WATER, AND THAT MOVEMENT MIXED THE FOOD COLORING FASTER. WHEN IT'S HOT OUTSIDE, THE AIR MOLECULES MOVE FASTER. THIS MEANS THAT SMELLS MIX FASTER AND MOVE FARTHER, SO IT'S ALWAYS EASIER TO SMELL SCENTS WHEN IT'S HOT OUTSIDE THAN WHEN IT'S COLD!

CHLOE, AGE 4, TRIED A VERY HOT CUP OF WATER, A CUP OF WATER AT ROOM TEMPERATURE, A COLD CUP OF WATER, AND AN ICY COLD CUP OF WATER. SHE WAS SURPRISED TO FIND THAT THE FOOD COLORING SPREAD THE FASTEST IN THE VERY HOT CUP AND THE SLOWEST IN THE COLD CUP.

ADVANCED LEVEL: What other questions do you have about temperature and how fast something spreads (diffusion)? Design an experiment to answer a question.

EXPLORE: PAINTING WITH WATERCOLORS, WATER, AND SALT

Using several squares of paper, try different amounts of water and different amounts of salt to see what patterns you can create. You can make watercolors to paint by adding 5 drops of food coloring to 1 teaspoon of water or by using liquid watercolors.

MATERIALS

- ☐ Paper squares (watercolor paper is best)
- ☐ Salt
- ☐ Watercolors
- ☐ Paintbrush

HELPFUL HINTS

- If you change just one thing at a time, it's easier to tell what that change does.

Extensions

USE WHAT YOU'VE LEARNED TO CREATE A WATERCOLOR AND SALT MASTERPIECE!

EXPLORE: WHAT MARKER COLORS ARE MADE OF

Many marker colors are created by mixing other colors together (for example, green can be made by mixing blue and yellow together). Using a process to separate colors into their individual pieces, called chromatography, you can see which colors were mixed together. Chromatography works when water moves up filter paper with a color marked on it and starts pushing the color molecules when it gets to them. Some color molecules are heavier than others, so the water will move them more slowly. As the water pushes the color molecules of your marker, you'll start to see the heavier color molecules separate from the lighter color molecules and you'll be able to see which colors were mixed to create the marker color you used. Test a variety of marker colors to see what happens. You can also try a variety of techniques to see what works best to separate the colors.

MATERIALS

- ☐ White coffee filters
- ☐ Washable markers (Dollar Tree markers work well)
- ☐ Water
- ☐ Cups

HELPFUL HINTS

- First add your marker color (or colors) to your dry coffee filter. You can make a dot, a line, or some other mark.

- Next, add water to one part of your coffee filter. Do not get your marker color wet.

- Allow the water to travel through the filter paper. When the water hits the marker color, it will begin pushing it. Different color pigments weigh different amounts and the water will push lighter colors faster. This will start to separate out the colors on the filter paper.

- You can try a variety of methods (for example, full coffee filters or coffee filter strips). You can try having the water run up the coffee filter, across the coffee filter, or down the coffee filter. Just remember to never add water directly to your mark. The key is to have the water move through the mark and to have a damp part and a dry part on the coffee filter.

Extensions

USE CHROMATOGRAPHY TO DECORATE FULL COFFEE FILTERS AND USE THE FINISHED FILTERS TO MAKE ART, SUCH AS FLOWER PETALS.

EXPERIMENT: WHICH TYPE OF MILK SWIRLS THE LONGEST?

When you add soap to certain types of milk that have food coloring added, the milk and food coloring will begin to swirl and mix all on their own. However, this reaction will occur only with certain types of milk. Can you figure out which type of milk swirls the longest with dish soap?

Make your guess: Which type of milk do you think will react and swirl with food coloring and dish soap the longest?

MATERIALS

- [ ] Different types of milk (for example, 2%, whole, skim, half-and-half, almond, soy)
- [ ] Food coloring
- [ ] Shallow dish
- [ ] Cotton swabs
- [ ] Dish soap

THINGS TO CONSIDER WHEN RUNNING YOUR EXPERIMENT:

Remember that the only thing you are changing is the type of milk. All other things should stay the same!

- How much of each type of milk will you use?
- To set up the experiment, you'll need to add your milk to a shallow dish and add a few drops of food coloring (add more than one color to make it more colorful) near the center of the dish. To start the reaction, touch a cotton swab that has been dipped in dish soap to the center of the milk in the dish.
- How many drops of food coloring will you add each time?

DATA

- How will you measure how long the milk is reacting each time?

WHAT DID YOU LEARN FROM YOUR EXPERIMENT? WHAT HAPPENED? WHY DO YOU THINK IT HAPPENED?

Real-life application

FATS AND OILS ARE VERY HARD TO CLEAN FROM DISHES. ASK YOUR PARENTS HOW THEY GET AN OILY PAN CLEAN AND THEY WILL PROBABLY SAY THEY ADD SOAP! SOAP MOLECULES CAN BREAK UP FAT AND OIL MOLECULES. BREAKING UP THE FATS AND OILS MAKES WASHING AN OILY PAN EASIER AND IT MAKES THE PRETTY COLOR MIXING YOU SEE IN THE MILK REACTION.

SAMANTHA, AGE 5, FILLED A TRAY WITH EQUAL AMOUNTS OF WHOLE MILK, 2% MILK, HALF-AND-HALF, AND HEAVY WHIPPING CREAM. SHE FOUND THAT THE LONGEST-REACTING ONE WAS THE WHOLE MILK, FOLLOWED CLOSELY BY THE HALF-AND-HALF.

ADVANCED LEVEL: What other questions do you have about milk, food coloring, and soap? Design an experiment to answer a question.

153

CHALLENGE: BUILD A TALL SUGAR CUBE TOWER BEFORE IT DISSOLVES

Can you beat the clock and build a super tall sugar cube tower before the water dissolves it? As soon as you add a sugar cube to the water, the water travels up the cube and dissolves it. You'll have to work quickly and be creative about how you build the tower before it dissolves!

MISSION: Build the tallest sugar cube tower you can before the water dissolves it.

MATERIALS: Sugar cubes and a pan or tray with edge filled with about ½ inch of water (with optional food coloring added).

HELPFUL HINTS

- Try different sized bases for your structure if your towers are dissolving and crumbling too quickly.

Extensions

WHAT SORTS OF STRUCTURES LASTED THE LONGEST? WHICH DISSOLVED THE FASTEST? WHY DO YOU THINK THIS IS?

WHAT DID YOU NOTICE ABOUT THE WATER AND THE SUGAR CUBES?

WHAT HAPPENS OVER TIME TO THE DISSOLVED SUGAR CUBES? WHY?

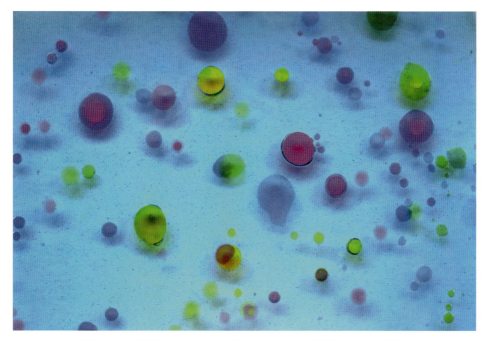

EXPLORE: OIL AND COLORED WATER

Fill a shallow tray with oil. Provide your child with several different containers of colored water and a pipette. You can make colored water for this activity by adding 5 drops of food coloring to 1 teaspoon of water or by using liquid watercolors. What do you notice as you add water to the oil? Can you suck the water back up using a pipette? Can you move the added water around the oil using a spoon or the tip of your pipette?

MATERIALS

☐ Shallow tray ☐ Cooking oil ☐ Colored water ☐ Pipettes

HELPFUL HINTS

- If you are able to put the oil in a clear-bottomed tray (plastic or glass), place it on top of white paper to see the colors even better.

Extensions

COLOR YOUR OIL BY ADDING A SMALL AMOUNT OF CANDY COLOR TO IT AND STIRRING WELL. WHAT DO YOU NOTICE? DOES THE COLOR OF THE OIL MIX WITH THE COLOR OF THE WATER? WHY DO YOU THINK THIS IS?

ADD SOME WATER AND OIL TO A SMALL CLEAR BOTTLE OR CONTAINER WITH A SEALING LID. SEAL THE LID TIGHTLY AND THEN SHAKE! WHAT DO YOU NOTICE? NOW LEAVE IT FOR 30 MINUTES. WHAT DO YOU NOTICE?

WHAT HAPPENS WHEN YOU ADD SOAP? WHY DO YOU THINK THIS HAPPENS?

CHALLENGE: MAKE THE HIGHEST-RISING DOUGH

What makes dough puff up? Can you design a recipe that makes the puffiest, highest-rising dough?

MISSION: Design the puffiest, highest-rising dough in the microwave using any combination of four ingredients.

MATERIALS

☐ Flour   ☐ Water   ☐ Baking soda   ☐ Baking powder

HELPFUL HINTS

- Try different amounts of water and different amounts of each ingredient. To maximize the puffiness, microwave just long enough for the dough to cook, about 10 to 30 seconds.

- Have an adult use the microwave and check the temperature of the dough once it's done puffing up. Pockets of steam can form and the dough can be very hot.

Extensions

CAN YOU TELL WHICH INGREDIENTS MADE YOUR DOUGH PUFF UP? CHECK SOME COOKBOOKS AT HOME (OR RECIPES ONLINE) THAT MAKE PUFFY BAKED GOODS, SUCH AS BREADS OR MUFFINS. DO YOU SEE THE SAME INGREDIENTS YOU TRIED? DO YOU SEE ANY OTHER INGREDIENTS YOU WANT TO TRY?

EXPLORE: BAKING SODA, BAKING POWDER, CORNSTARCH, FLOUR, SALT, AND SUGAR

Explore what happens to each substance when you mix it with others (such as warm water, cold water, oil, soap, cabbage juice, and vinegar). Make notes! You will use these notes in the next challenge activity to figure out which mystery substance you have.

MATERIALS

- ☐ Baking soda
- ☐ Baking powder
- ☐ Cornstarch
- ☐ Warm water
- ☐ Cold water
- ☐ Flour
- ☐ Salt
- ☐ Sugar
- ☐ Vinegar
- ☐ Spoons
- ☐ Oil
- ☐ Soap
- ☐ Red cabbage juice (see page 125)
- ☐ Cups

HELPFUL HINTS

- Remember if you mix just one thing at a time, it's easier to tell what that change does.

Extensions

SEE THE NEXT CHALLENGE ACTIVITY.

CHALLENGE: IDENTIFY
THE MYSTERY SUBSTANCE

Using what you learned in the last activity, can you experiment and tell what a mystery ingredient is?

MISSION: Identify a mystery substance.

MATERIALS

☐ A mystery substance chosen by an adult (salt, sugar, flour, cornstarch, or baking soda)

☐ Testing materials (warm water, cold water, cabbage juice, vinegar, or anything else you can think of!)

HELPFUL HINTS

- Look at any notes or pictures you drew from the previous activity for hints!

CHALLENGE: MAKE A CABBAGE JUICE RAINBOW

If you mix an ingredient with cabbage juice, it will always create a certain color. For example, cabbage juice always turns blue when you mix in baking soda. Different ingredients will make cabbage juice turn different colors. Can you find things that make cabbage juice turn every color of the rainbow? Can you get close?

MISSION: Try to make a rainbow of color using cabbage juice and household ingredients.

MATERIALS

- ☐ Red cabbage juice (see page 131)
- ☐ Pipette
- ☐ Any ingredient you can think of from your house

HELPFUL HINTS

- Try adding a variety of ingredients, both liquid and solid.
- Try adding ingredients from your laundry room and your kitchen.

Chapter 6
Baking Soda and Vinegar

INTRODUCTION

In this chapter you will explore some simple chemical reactions that use baking soda to make bubbles! Baking soda is usually white and vinegar and citric acid are clear, but to make it more fun, we added colors to ours. If you'd like to color your vinegar, just add a few drops of food coloring or liquid watercolors and give it a good stir. If you want to make colored baking soda, add a teaspoon of water mixed with food coloring or liquid watercolors for every cup of baking soda you are using and mix it into the baking soda really well. Leave it out to dry and in about one day, you'll have dry colored baking soda to experiment with!

SIMPLE EXPLANATION

Adding certain things to baking soda will make the baking soda chemical break into pieces. When this happens, one of the things the baking soda breaks into is gas. This means that the baking soda mixture will bubble! The gas bubbles let you know it is reacting, or breaking apart and changing into other chemicals.

This chemical reaction is safe to touch with your hands and safe to wash down the sink when you're done.

LONGER EXPLANATION

When you mix two or more chemicals together and they break apart and rearrange to form new and different chemicals, we call that a chemical reaction. When you mix baking soda and vinegar together, they break apart and rearrange to form a gas, water, and a new chemical (that looks a lot like baking soda, but is actually sodium acetate!). All of the starting materials and ending products here are safe to touch with your hands. (But avoid getting it in your eyes, as it does sting a bit.)

In some of the activities in this chapter, you will have a chance to explore the chemical reaction between baking soda and citric acid. Citric acid is used as a preservative when canning food and is also added to some candies to increase the tangy sour taste. It is naturally found in citrus fruits, such as lemons (and thus is found in lemon juice). It is also an ingredient in Kool-Aid powdered drink mix. When you mix baking soda and citric acid, they break apart and rearrange to form gas, water, and sodium citrate. Like the chemicals in the baking soda and vinegar reaction, all of these ingredients are safe to touch. However, it might irritate your skin if you make the citric acid concentration too high, so be sure to mix it with a good amount of water if you plan to touch it.

These chemical reactions are some of our favorites because the gas that forms makes bubbles very quickly and it's fun to watch. We like to add soap to our vinegar (or citric acid) before adding it to baking soda. When soapy vinegar (or citric acid) is added to baking soda it holds the gasses inside the soap and makes a huge pile of bubbles!

The chemical reactions between baking soda and vinegar and between baking soda and citric acid are permanent. This means that once the baking soda and vinegar (or the baking soda and citric acid) finish reacting, there won't be any more bubbling. Even though the sodium acetate (produced with vinegar) and the sodium citrate (produced with citric acid) look like baking soda, they are actually different chemicals and won't make bubbles if you mix them with vinegar.

Both sodium acetate and sodium citrate are safe to rinse down the sink.

SUPPLY LIST FOR THE ACTIVITIES IN THIS CHAPTER
- [ ] Baking soda
- [ ] Vinegar
- [ ] Dish soap
- [ ] Shampoo
- [ ] Hand soap
- [ ] Sandwich-sized ziplock bags
- [ ] Tall plastic cups
- [ ] Permanent marker
- [ ] Salt
- [ ] Lemon juice

- [ ] Measuring cups and spoons
- [ ] Pipettes
- [ ] Cookie sheet or other shallow baking tray
- [ ] Balloons
- [ ] Foam sheets
- [ ] Plastic bottle with small opening, such as a water bottle
- [ ] Food coloring (optional) or liquid watercolors (optional)
- [ ] Kool-Aid powder packets (optional)
- [ ] Citric acid powder (optional)

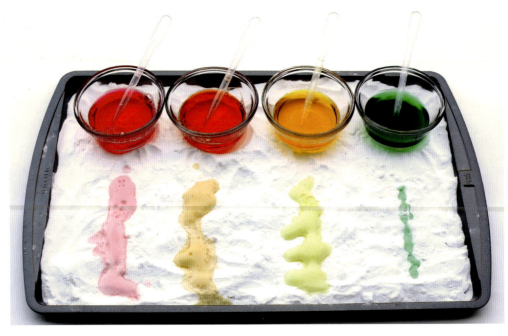

EXPLORE: BAKING SODA REACTION TRAY

In this activity you'll get to explore how baking soda reacts with more things. What happens when you add each thing? What do you think is happening? What happens if you mix some of the liquids together and then add them?

SET UP

Fill a shallow tray with baking soda. Explore the different containers of soapy vinegar, soapy water, soapy lemon juice, soapy Kool-Aid, or soapy citric acid.

MATERIALS

☐ Shallow tray   ☐ Baking soda   ☐ Vinegar

☐ Soap   ☐ Lemon juice   ☐ Water

☐ Kool-Aid powder packet dissolved in water (optional)

☐ Citric acid powder dissolved in water (optional)

HELPFUL HINTS

- Add color to each to more easily identify which one is which on the tray.

Extensions

CAN YOU THINK OF A WAY TO TEST WHICH REACTION PRODUCES THE MOST GAS? (HINT: SEE THE CHALLENGE ACTIVITY ON PAGE 167)

IS THERE ANYTHING ELSE THAT YOU WOULD LIKE TO TRY TESTING WITH BAKING SODA?

EXPERIMENT: WHICH SOAP WILL MAKE THE TALLEST MOUNTAIN OF BUBBLES?

Adding soap to baking soda and vinegar will create bubbles as the soap traps the gas created inside bubbles of soap. But do all soaps make the same amount of bubbles, or is there a soap that will make more bubbles?

MAKE YOUR GUESS: Which kind of soap (for example, shampoo, bubble bath, body wash, hand soap, dish soap, laundry soap) do you think will make the tallest mountain of bubbles when you add it to baking soda and vinegar?

THINGS TO CONSIDER WHEN RUNNING YOUR EXPERIMENT

Remember that the only thing you are changing is which soap you are adding to which. All other things should stay the same!

- What amount of baking soda will you use each time?
- What amount of vinegar?
- What amount of soap?
- Will you add the soap to the baking soda or to the vinegar?

DATA

- How will you measure the size of the reaction?

WHAT DID YOU LEARN FROM YOUR EXPERIMENT? WHAT HAPPENED? WHY DO YOU THINK IT HAPPENED?

JON, AGE 5, ADDED 2 TEASPOONS OF BAKING SODA TO EACH VASE. HE ADDED 1 TABLESPOON OF BUBBLE BATH TO ONE VASE, 1 TABLESPOON OF HAND SOAP TO ANOTHER, AND 1 TABLESPOON OF FOAMING HAND SOAP TO THE LAST VASE. AFTER ADDING 1/4 CUP OF VINEGAR, HE WATCHED HOW FAR THE BUBBLES TRAVELED ON THE TRAY TO DECIDE WHICH SOAP MADE THE TALLEST MOUNTAIN OF BUBBLES. HE FOUND THAT THE HAND SOAP MADE THE MOST BUBBLES!

ADVANCED LEVEL: What other questions do you have about adding things to a baking soda and vinegar reaction? Design an experiment to answer a question.

CHALLENGE: FIND THE SMALLEST AMOUNT OF BAKING SODA NEEDED TO POP A BAG

If you add baking soda to a ziplock bag filled with ½ cup of vinegar (and a squirt of soap for fun) and quickly seal it, it might produce enough gas to pop the bag! Can you find the smallest amount of baking soda needed to pop a ziplock bag filled with ½ cup of vinegar and a squirt of soap?

MISSION: Find the smallest amount of baking soda needed to pop a ziplock bag filled with ½ cup of vinegar.

MATERIALS

- ☐ Ziplock sandwich bags
- ☐ Dish soap (optional)
- ☐ Baking soda
- ☐ Paper towel or tissue paper
- ☐ Vinegar
- ☐ Measuring cups and spoons

HELPFUL HINTS

- Either start with a lot of baking soda and work your way down, or start with a small amount and work your way up. You can rinse and reuse your ziplock bag if it doesn't pop.
- You don't want to mix the baking soda and vinegar before you close the bag. If you do, some of the gas you are producing will escape. Try wrapping the baking soda in a piece of paper towel, tissue, or tissue paper. Seal the bag and then gently shake it to mix the baking soda and the soapy vinegar.
- Please wear eye protection.
- Note that depending on how forcefully the bag explodes, there is the potential for sodium acetate, soap, and water to get on the surroundings. It cleans easily, but keep this in mind when deciding where to do the activity!

Extensions

TRY THIS SAME ACTIVITY IN A LARGER BAG WITH MORE VINEGAR. (NOTE: IN PHOTO, WE USED A GALLON-SIZED ZIPLOCK BAG.)

CHALLENGE: MAKE THE TALLEST REACTION OF BAKING SODA IN A CUP

What amounts and combinations of ingredients will make the tallest reaction of a tablespoon of baking soda?

MISSION: Make the tallest reaction of 1 tablespoon of baking soda using any combination of ingredients.

MATERIALS

- [ ] Large plastic cup
- [ ] Permanent marker
- [ ] Baking soda
- [ ] Vinegar
- [ ] Water
- [ ] Soap
- [ ] Shampoo
- [ ] Salt
- [ ] Lemon juice
- [ ] Anything else you want to try!

HELPFUL HINTS

- Mark the highest point of your eruption each time by making a line on the cup with your permanent marker.

Extensions

WHAT HAPPENS WHEN YOU REMOVE ONE SET OF INGREDIENTS YOU USED TO MAKE THE TALLEST ERUPTION? CAN YOU FIGURE OUT WHAT EACH INGREDIENT DOES?

EXPERIMENT: SHOULD YOU ADD BAKING SODA TO VINEGAR OR VICE VERSA TO MAKE A BIGGER REACTION?

Does the order matter? If you want a big reaction, should you add your baking soda to a container of vinegar or your vinegar to a container of baking soda? Or does it not make a difference?

MAKE YOUR GUESS: Do you think adding baking soda to vinegar or adding vinegar to baking soda will make a bigger reaction?

THINGS TO CONSIDER WHEN RUNNING YOUR EXPERIMENT

Remember that the only thing you are changing is the order of which you are adding to which. All other things should stay the same!

- What amount of baking soda will you use each time?
- What amount of vinegar?

DATA

- How will you measure the size of the reaction?

WHAT DID YOU LEARN FROM YOUR EXPERIMENT? WHAT HAPPENED? WHY DO YOU THINK IT HAPPENED?

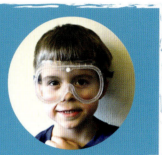

JON, AGE 5, ADDED 1/4 CUP OF VINEGAR TO 2 TABLESPOONS OF BAKING SODA IN A PLASTIC CUP AT THE SAME TIME THAT HE ADDED 2 TABLESPOONS OF BAKING SODA TO 1/4 CUP OF VINEGAR IN A PLASTIC CUP. IT WAS HARD TO TELL WHICH REACTION WAS BIGGER, BUT HE THINKS IT WAS THE ONE IN WHICH HE ADDED BAKING SODA TO THE VINEGAR IN A PLASTIC CUP. HE WANTS TO TRY AGAIN WITH DIFFERENT AMOUNTS OF BAKING SODA AND VINEGAR TO SEE WHAT HAPPENS.

ADVANCED LEVEL: What other questions do you have about adding baking soda to vinegar or vice versa? Design an experiment to answer a question.

EXPLORE: MAKE FIZZING BAKING SODA PAINT

Can you make baking soda paint by mixing baking soda with either liquid watercolors or food coloring and water? What does it look like when you paint it on paper? What happens if you spray vinegar on your painting? What if you add vinegar to your painting with a pipette? What if you add vinegar with a paintbrush? What if you add vinegar to the paper and then paint over it with baking soda paint?

MATERIALS

- ☐ Vinegar ☐ Baking soda ☐ Paintbrush ☐ Pipette
- ☐ Liquid watercolors or food coloring and water ☐ A spray bottle

HELPFUL HINTS

- Baking soda tends to settle, so you may need to briefly stir before painting each time.
- Place your paper on top of paper towels while painting to help contain any overflow from your paintings.

CHALLENGE: FIND THE RIGHT AMOUNT OF VINEGAR TO REACT WITH BAKING SODA

Can you find the exact amount of vinegar needed to react with 2 teaspoons of baking soda? If you add too little vinegar, some baking soda will be left. If you add too much vinegar, nothing will happen because all the baking soda will have reacted and there won't be any baking soda left.

MISSION: Can you find the exact amount of vinegar it takes to fully react with 2 teaspoons of baking soda?

MATERIALS

☐ Baking soda   ☐ Vinegar   ☐ Soap (optional)

☐ Cup   ☐ Measuring spoons   ☐ Pipettes

HELPFUL HINTS

- You can use pipettes or measuring spoons to measure small amounts of vinegar.

Extensions

EXACTLY HOW MUCH LEMON JUICE DOES IT TAKE TO FULLY REACT WITH 2 TEASPOONS OF BAKING SODA?

CAN YOU FIND THE EXACT AMOUNT OF VINEGAR OR LEMON JUICE NEEDED FOR ANOTHER AMOUNT OF BAKING SODA?

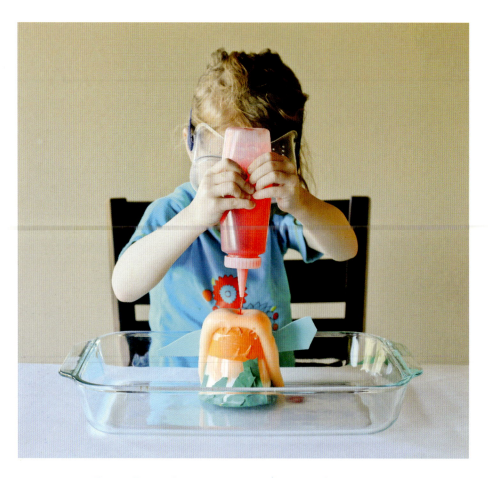

CHALLENGE: DESIGN AN ERUPTING VOLCANO

Baking soda and vinegar are often used together to simulate the eruption of lava from a volcano. For this challenge you get to create your own volcano and then use what you know about baking soda and vinegar to make a fantastic eruption of pretend lava bubbles! Will you make a big or small volcano, a tall and thin volcano, or a short and wide volcano? It's up to you!

MISSION: Build a volcano from the supplies you have. Then test your design by erupting your pretend lava!

MATERIALS

- ☐ Scissors
- ☐ Plastic cups
- ☐ Baking soda
- ☐ Vinegar
- ☐ Soap
- ☐ Foam sheets
- ☐ Masking tape
- ☐ Anything else you can think of!

HELPFUL HINTS

- Foam sheets and masking tape hold up well to moisture. Your lava will be wet, so choose your building materials with that in mind.
- Adding a few squirts of soap to your vinegar will make a puffier, foamier eruption of pretend lava.

Extensions

CAN YOU ERUPT YOUR VOLCANO WITH SOMETHING OTHER THAN VINEGAR?

IS YOUR VOLCANO REUSABLE? IF NOT, CAN YOU THINK OF ANOTHER DESIGN THAT WOULD BE?

MAKE TWO DIFFERENT SHAPED OR DIFFERENT SIZED VOLCANOES AND COMPARE THE SPEED AND SIZE OF THE ERUPTIONS.

EXPERIMENT: DO FROZEN AND DRIED BAKING SODA REACT DIFFERENTLY?

Does baking soda react differently if we freeze it or if we dry it? Which reaction will be faster? Or will they both react at the same speed?

MAKE YOUR GUESS: Which do you think will react faster when added to vinegar: frozen baking soda and water or dried baking soda and water?

THINGS TO CONSIDER WHEN RUNNING YOUR EXPERIMENT:

Remember that the only thing you are changing is whether the baking soda is dried or frozen. All other things should stay the same!

- How much baking soda and water will you use? (Hint: using 3 to 5 teaspoons of water per 1 cup of baking soda will make a type of dough you can roll into a ball that will then dry or freeze)
- How long will you allow the baking soda and water to freeze or dry?
- How much vinegar will you add it to?

DATA

- How will you measure how quickly it reacts?

WHAT DID YOU LEARN FROM YOUR EXPERIMENT? WHAT HAPPENED? WHY DO YOU THINK IT HAPPENED?

ELSIE, AGE 6, USED HAND-ROLLED BALLS MADE OF 1/2 CUP OF BAKING SODA TO 3 TEASPOONS OF GREEN WATER. ONE WAS FROZEN OVERNIGHT AND THE OTHER DRIED ON THE COUNTER OVERNIGHT. SHE FOUND THAT FROZEN BAKING SODA HAD A FASTER REACTION AND A LONGER REACTION THAN DRIED BAKING SODA.

ADVANCED LEVEL: What other questions do you have about dried or frozen baking soda? Design an experiment to answer a question.

CHALLENGE: BLOW UP A BALLOON WITH BAKING SODA AND VINEGAR, BUT DON'T POP IT!

Fill up an empty water bottle with some amount of vinegar, then place a baking soda-filled balloon over the mouth of the bottle. Once it's sealed, if you shake the baking soda out of the balloon, the gas created will blow up the balloon. Can you find an amount of baking soda and vinegar that will blow the balloon up a lot, but not pop it?

MISSION: Find the right amount of baking soda and vinegar needed to blow up a balloon, but not pop it!

MATERIALS

☐ Balloon   ☐ Empty plastic bottle   ☐ Baking soda   ☐ Vinegar

HELPFUL HINTS

- If you'd like to avoid hearing too many popped balloons, start with small amounts of baking soda and vinegar.

Extensions

CAN YOU BLOW UP A BALLOON WITH LEMON JUICE AND BAKING SODA? HOW MUCH OF EACH INGREDIENT DO YOU NEED?

WHAT ABOUT KOOL-AID AND BAKING SODA? HOW MUCH OF EACH?

EXPLORE: HOW FREEZING CHANGES THE REACTION BETWEEN BAKING SODA AND VINEGAR

Find out how frozen vinegar reacts with baking soda at room temperature. Is it different from how frozen baking soda reacts with vinegar at room temperature? How does freezing baking soda or vinegar change how quickly they react?

MATERIALS:

☐ Vinegar ☐ Water ☐ Baking soda ☐ Various shaped containers ☐ Tray

HELPFUL HINTS:

- Plan for at least four hours to freeze each item.
- Mix a small amount of water with the baking soda to make it easier to freeze. Be sure to use the same amount of water each time!
- Be sure you compare the same amounts of baking soda and vinegar each time.

Extensions

WHICH REACTION DID YOU LIKE BEST? CAN YOU THINK OF SOMETHING ELSE YOU'D LIKE TO TRY?

WHY DO YOU THINK THEY DO DIFFERENT THINGS?

Chapter 7

Environmental Science

INTRODUCTION

The things we do every day can have an effect on the plants and animals in our environment. In this chapter we'll learn more about problems our behavior can cause for the world around us. From car washes to salting our sidewalks to making sure we stay on marked trails when hiking, there's a lot we can do to lessen our impact on the planet.

RECOMMENDED MATERIALS FOR THIS CHAPTER

- ☐ Plants (see page 31 for information on how to grow your own)
- ☐ Dish soap
- ☐ Empty 2 liter plastic soda bottles
- ☐ Rocks
- ☐ Coffee filters
- ☐ Cotton balls
- ☐ Paper towels
- ☐ Soil
- ☐ Ziplock bags
- ☐ Salt
- ☐ Feathers
- ☐ Cooking oil or mineral oil
- ☐ Foil
- ☐ Straws

- ☐ Spray bottle with water
- ☐ Food coloring
- ☐ Tray or dish with sides
- ☐ DIY root viewer (page 52)
- ☐ Fallen leaves or shredded newspaper
- ☐ Non-citrus fruit cores, rinds, or peels
- ☐ Black foam sheets
- ☐ Sticky-back velcro
- ☐ Redworms

EXPERIMENT: HOW DOES POLLUTION CHANGE PLANT GROWTH?

Pollution is anything added to the environment (the living world around you) that can cause harm. People often unknowingly add pollution to their environment. What happens when you wash your car in your driveway? Could that cause harm to plant life in your environment?

MAKE YOUR GUESS: How do you think different amounts of pollution (soap) will change plant growth?

THINGS TO CONSIDER WHEN RUNNING YOUR EXPERIMENT:

Remember that the only thing you are changing is the amount of pollution (soap). All other things should stay the same!

- What amounts of pollution (soap) will you try?
- How long will you run your experiment for?
- How big will your plants be before you start the experiment?

DATA

- How will you measure the effect of the pollution?
- How long will you run your experiment?

WHAT DID YOU LEARN FROM YOUR EXPERIMENT? WHAT HAPPENED? WHY DO YOU THINK IT HAPPENED?

Real-life application

POLLUTION COMES IN MANY FORMS, INCLUDING SOAP AND OTHER DETERGENTS. RUNOFF FROM WASHING CARS AT HOUSES CAN AFFECT PLANTS AND ANIMALS BECAUSE IT GOES TO STORM DRAINS AND THEN TO STREAMS AND RIVERS AND ULTIMATELY THE OCEAN. COMMERCIAL CAR WASHES HAVE SPECIAL DRAINS THAT COLLECT THE SOAPY RUNOFF AND CARRY IT TO A WATER TREATMENT PLANT.

LUKE, AGE 7, TESTED FOUR PLANTS. HE ADDED 40 ML OF PLAIN WATER TO ONE PLANT, 1/2 TEASPOON OF SOAP MIXED WITH 40 ML OF WATER TO ANOTHER, 1 TEASPOON OF SOAP MIXED WITH 40 ML TO ANOTHER, AND 1 TABLESPOON OF SOAP MIXED WITH 40 ML TO THE LAST PLANT. WITHIN A WEEK, THE PLANTS WITH 1 TEASPOON AND 1 TABLESPOON OF SOAP ADDED TO THE WATER WERE DYING.

ADVANCED LEVEL: What other questions do you have about plants and pollution? Design an experiment to answer a question.

CHALLENGE: PURIFY WATER

All the water that ever will be already exists here on Earth. This makes it even more important to clean or purify polluted (dirty) water. Can you design a system to purify cloudy water?

MISSION: Can you design a system that will purify cloudy water?

MATERIALS

- [ ] One-liter plastic bottle
- [ ] Rocks
- [ ] Cloudy water (made by stirring some fine dirt into tap water)
- [ ] Cotton balls
- [ ] Paper towels
- [ ] Coffee filters
- [ ] Anything else you can think of!

DIRECTIONS

1. Have an adult cut off the top third of a plastic bottle.
2. Remove the lid.
3. Flip the top upside down so that it creates a funnel.
4. Add items to your funnel to filter water.
5. Once you have the filter set up inside your funnel, pour the water through and allow it to collect in the bottle's base.

HELPFUL HINTS

- Depending on the design of your filter, you might need to wait for quite a while for the water to make its way through.
- Compare the filtered water collected in the base to the original water. Did you get it cleaner?

Extensions

TRY POLLUTING YOUR WATER IN OTHER WAYS. DOES YOUR FILTER WORK EQUALLY WELL?

IF YOUR FILTER HAS MANY PARTS, WHICH PART DO YOU THINK WORKED THE BEST? WHAT HAPPENS IF YOU MAKE A FILTER USING JUST THAT PART?

EXPERIMENT: WHAT WILL DECOMPOSE FIRST IN SOIL?

When something decomposes, it breaks down into its smallest parts. Dead leaves and plants decompose and create new healthy soil for future plants. Decomposition is an important process. Can you imagine what the world would look like if every dead leaf or plant that ever existed were still around? One environmental problem that people cause is our creation of items that do not decompose. Some of the things you throw away in your garbage might sit in a landfill (where garbage goes) for hundreds of years! Choose several items from your house and put them to the test. Which will decompose first?

MAKE YOUR GUESS: Which of the items you chose do you think will decompose first?

THINGS TO CONSIDER WHEN RUNNING YOUR EXPERIMENT

Remember that the only thing you are changing is the type of item you're adding to the soil. All other things should stay the same!

- Remember to keep the size of the items about the same.
- Because of smell, I recommend avoiding meats and other proteins. Fruits and vegetables are less smelly.
- Try to use both food scraps and man-made items (for example, cardboard or plastic).
- You can use either a ziplock bag or a root viewer for this experiment.
- Make sure you add water to help the process of decomposition.

DATA

- How will you decide whether something is decomposing or not?

WHAT DID YOU LEARN FROM YOUR EXPERIMENT? WHAT HAPPENED? WHY DO YOU THINK IT HAPPENED?

Real-life application

MANY CITIES HAVE A COMPOSTING PROGRAM FOR GARBAGE ITEMS THAT DO DECOMPOSE. WHY DO YOU THINK WE TRY TO RECYCLE CERTAIN ITEMS? WHAT DO YOU THINK HAPPENS TO THE ITEMS YOU EXPERIMENTED WITH IN A LANDFILL (WHERE THE GARBAGE TRUCKS TAKE YOUR GARBAGE)?

AMELIA, AGE 4, AND ROBBY, AGE 4, PLACED A ROCK, A LEGO FIGURINE, A LEAF, A PIPE CLEANER, A TOILET PAPER ROLL, AND A CRACKER IN ZIPLOCK BAGS WITH WET SOIL. THEY FOUND THAT AFTER A WEEK, THE TOILET PAPER ROLL AND CRACKER HAD GOTTEN MUSHY AND THE LEAF HAD TURNED BROWN. THE PIPE CLEANER, ROCK, AND LEGO FIGURINE STILL LOOKED THE SAME.

ADVANCED LEVEL: What other questions do you have about decomposition? Design an experiment to answer a question.

CHALLENGE: REDUCE EROSION

Erosion is when rain carries dirt down to streams, rivers, and oceans. Can you design ways to reduce erosion? Keeping the water that goes to streams, rivers, and oceans clean and clear rather than cloudy is important for the health of the creatures, like fish, that live in those places.

MISSION: Design a system to reduce the amount of soil that erodes when it rains.

MATERIALS

☐ Two-liter plastic bottles

☐ A container or cup to catch the draining water

☐ Soil

☐ Plants

- [ ] Sticks
- [ ] Small rocks
- [ ] Anything else you can think of!
- [ ] A spray or squeeze bottle with water to represent the rain

DIRECTIONS

1. Have an adult cut off one side of two or more 2-liter bottles. (Note: Because of the thickness of the bottles at the base and the top, it is easiest to cut slightly less than half a side off of the bottles and leave the very top and very bottom of the bottles intact.)
2. Remove the lids.
3. Lay the bottles on their sides.
4. Fill each of the bottles with the same amount of soil.
5. Leave one bottle as soil, but add things to the other bottle(s) to try to stop erosion.
6. Once you have your bottles set up, add the same amount of "rain" water to each and then tip them and collect the runoff water from each in an individual cup or container.

HELPFUL HINTS

- Compare the cloudiness of the drained water to see how successful each of your models was at keeping dirt from leaving with the rain.

Extensions

IF YOU HAVE HILLS NEAR YOUR HOUSE, TAKE A FIELD TRIP TO SEE HOW PEOPLE HAVE WORKED TO STOP THEM FROM ERODING. DID YOU TRY SOMETHING LIKE THIS IN ONE OF YOUR MODELS? IF NOT, DOES IT GIVE YOU AN IDEA FOR SOMETHING TO TRY?

EXPLORE: BUILD A WATERSHED

Did you know that you live in a watershed? A watershed is the name for the area of land
where all the water leads to the same place. All the rain in your watershed might go to a
river, lake, or ocean. Every watershed is different. For this activity, you get to build a pretend
watershed out of paper and straws and tape and cover it with foil. Add rain (water sprayed
from a water bottle) and watch what happens to your rain. Does it form a river? A lake?

MATERIALS

- [ ] Paper
- [ ] Straws
- [ ] Tape
- [ ] Foil
- [ ] Spray bottle with water
- [ ] Food coloring (optional)
- [ ] A dish or tray with an edge

HELPFUL HINTS

- Use crumpled paper, tape, and straws to construct hills or mountains. Be sure to cover all of your "land" with foil so the "rain" won't soak in.

- Once all of your land is covered with foil, spray water from a water bottle to make rain. Does your rain form rivers? A lake?

- If your water gathers all in one place, you have one watershed. If it gathers in several places you've made several watersheds.

- To see how pollution changes a watershed, add a drop of food coloring somewhere on your land. Add rain. What happens to the pollution? Where does it end up?

Real-life application

FIND OUT WHAT YOUR WATERSHED IS CALLED AND WHERE YOUR WATER ENDS UP (FOR EXAMPLE, A RIVER, LAKE, OR OCEAN).

TAKE A WALK OUTSIDE OF YOUR HOUSE AND PAY ATTENTION TO THE SIDES OF THE STREETS (OR GUTTERS IF YOU LIVE WHERE THERE ARE SIDEWALKS). DO YOU NOTICE BIG DRAINS? THOSE ARE STORM DRAINS AND THEY HELP MOVE THE WATER FROM YOUR NEIGHBORHOOD TO WHEREVER YOUR WATERSHED ENDS. THIS MEANS IF YOU HAVE TRASH OR CHEMICALS ON THE STREET AT YOUR HOUSE, IT WILL EVENTUALLY END UP IN A RIVER, LAKE, OR OCEAN! THIS IS WHY IT IS SO IMPORTANT TO KEEP OUR STORM DRAINS CLEAR OF GARBAGE AND POLLUTANTS.

IF THE STORM DRAINS IN YOUR COMMUNITY AREN'T LABELED, CONTACT YOUR CITY TO SEE IF YOU CAN START A PROGRAM. THERE ARE MANY DIFFERENT WAYS TO MARK DRAINS TO RAISE AWARENESS ABOUT WHERE THE WATER GOES, FROM PLAQUES TO STENCILS.

EXPERIMENT: DOES SALT CHANGE PLANT GROWTH?

Businesses and houses often add salt to sidewalks in the winter to melt ice. When the ice melts, it carries the salt with it. What do you think this added salt does to nearby plants?

MAKE YOUR GUESS: Do you think salt will change how well plants grow?

THINGS TO CONSIDER WHEN RUNNING YOUR EXPERIMENT

Remember that the only thing you are changing is the amount of salt you add. All other things should stay the same!

- How many different amounts of salt will you try?
- How big will your plants be when you start the experiment?
- How long will you run your experiment?

DATA

- How will you measure plant growth?
- How often will you check?

WHAT DID YOU LEARN FROM YOUR EXPERIMENT? WHAT HAPPENED? WHY DO YOU THINK IT HAPPENED?

Real-life application

DO YOU ADD ANYTHING TO YOUR DRIVEWAY OR SIDEWALKS WHEN THEY ARE FROZEN? WHAT ABOUT YOUR CITY?

WHAT DO YOU THINK THE ADDED SALT DOES TO NEARBY WILDLIFE, ESPECIALLY THE FISH AND SMALL BUGS THAT LIVE IN NEARBY STREAMS, RIVERS, AND LAKES?

Extension

MAGNESIUM CHLORIDE IS A SAFER SALT FOR DE-ICING SIDEWALKS. BUY SOME AND TRY RUNNING THE SAME EXPERIMENT TO SEE IF THE EFFECTS ARE THE SAME.

MARSHALL, AGE 4, CHOSE FOUR PLANTS. HE ADDED 40 ML OF WATER TO ONE, 40 ML OF WATER WITH 1 TEASPOON OF SALT TO ANOTHER, 40 ML OF WATER WITH 4 TEASPOONS OF SALT TO ANOTHER, AND 40 ML OF WATER WITH 12 TEASPOONS OF SALT TO THE LAST ONE. HE FOUND THAT THE PLANTS WITH SALT DIED WITHIN TWO DAYS!

ADVANCED LEVEL: What other questions do you have about salt and plants? Design an experiment to answer a question.

EXPLORE: OIL-COATED FEATHERS

When oil spills in nature, birds often become coated in oil. Oil spills often have devastating effects on birds and other wildlife. In this activity, you'll combine feathers, oil, and water. Compare the oil-covered feathers to dry feathers. How are they different? Can you get the feathers clean again?

MATERIALS

- ☐ Feathers
- ☐ Oil (for example, cooking oil, olive oil, mineral oil)
- ☐ Soap
- ☐ Water
- ☐ Tray
- ☐ Cups

HELPFUL HINTS

- If possible, try two types of feathers (you can find different types of feathers at craft stores, such as long, thin wing feathers and shorter, fluffier body feathers).

Extensions

WATCH A VIDEO OR LOOK UP INFORMATION ON HOW OIL SPILLS AFFECT BIRDS.

EXPLORE: OBSERVE REDWORMS

Redworms are very popular additions to home compost bins. They take our fruit and vegetable food waste (such as peels, cores, rinds) and break it down into healthy soil that can be used to grow plants. Redworms can compost, or break down, approximately 3 times their weight in food per week! In this activity, you'll create a worm viewer so you can take a sneak peek at what goes on in a compost bin.

MATERIALS

- ☐ Redworms
- ☐ Spray bottle
- ☐ Damp fallen leaves or dampened shredded print newspaper
- ☐ Root viewer (see page 52)
- ☐ Lettuce or other leaves
- ☐ Sticky-backed Velcro pieces
- ☐ Non-citrus fruit
- ☐ Two black foam sheets

DIRECTIONS

1. Make a viewer according to the steps on page 52.

2. Measure and cut two 8-by-10-inch pieces of black foam.

3. Affix sticky-backed Velcro piecesto each corner of the two pieces of black foam.

4. Gently press one Velcro-affixed piece of black foam to the front of the viewer and one to the back of the viewer.

5. Collect damp fallen leaves from outside. If you don't have access to damp fallen leaves, dampen shredded black and white print (not color) newspaper.

6. Add a layer (about 2 inches) of damp leaves or newspaper to the bottom of your root viewer.

7. Add a layer (about 2 inches) of green weeds, grass, or old lettuce.

8. Add a layer of non-citrus fruit (rinds, cores, or peels are fine).

9. Add a final layer (about 2 inches) of damp leaves or newspaper to the top.

10. Place a sheet of dry paper or newspaper over the top of your viewer. This will help deter fruit flies.

11. Add your redworms. This setup will accommodate a maximum of 50 worms.

12. Place in a warm location (examples include under your sink or in your garage) and check it every few days to see if your worms need water or more "food."

HELPFUL HINTS

- The worms should have a moist, but not wet environment. When checking on the viewer, you should be able to see moisture along the front and back walls. If you do not, using a spray bottle, add 3–5 sprays of water to the top of your viewer.

- Worms will avoid eating the rinds of citrus fruits, so I recommend using non-citrus fruits only for the best results.

- Colored newspaper may have inks that are harmful to worms; I recommend using black and white print newspaper if you don't have access to fallen leaves.

Extensions

USE THE SOIL YOUR WORMS CREATE TO GROW STRAWBERRIES, OR ANOTHER FOOD-PRODUCING PLANT.

Chapter 8

Living Things

INTRODUCTION

Insects are great subjects for science experiments. However, they are living creatures, and it is important to treat them with kindness and respect. Please always handle them gently, and if you are using insects for your experiments, please return them to their natural homes when your experiment is done. If you are keeping insects for more than one day, be sure that they have a water source (a damp pom pom or cotton ball works well). If you are keeping insects for two days or more, please be sure they have a food source.

If you live in an area where it's difficult to find insects, Appendix A includes suggestions on where to purchase them.

All living things need food, shelter, air, and water, but each type of insect will have individual preferences. In the experiments in these chapters, you will get to discover what sorts of things your insects like. It is important to never set up experiments that could harm your insects. Please always check with an adult to be sure that the things you'd like to try are safe for your insects.

Insects that work well for the experiments you will find here include isopods (also known as pill bugs, roly-polies, or potato bugs), crickets, caterpillars, ladybugs, and praying mantises.

RECOMMENDED MATERIALS LIST

- [ ] Butterfly kit
- [ ] Praying mantis egg case
- [ ] Boxes
- [ ] Paper

- ☐ Tape
- ☐ Paper towels
- ☐ Cups
- ☐ Plastic wrap
- ☐ Insects (such as crickets, ladybugs, and isopods)
- ☐ Pom poms or cotton balls
- ☐ Slug or snail
- ☐ Glue stick

EXPERIMENT: IS SLUG (OR SNAIL) SLIME AS STRONG AS A GLUE STICK?

Snails and slugs can use the slime they create to stick to different surfaces, even very smooth surfaces like glass. Their slime is strong enough to allow them to crawl upside down on plant leaves and other surfaces without falling. Just how strong is their slime? Do you think slug (or snail) slime is stronger than a glue stick?

MAKE YOUR GUESS: Is slug (or snail) slime as strong as a glue stick?

THINGS TO CONSIDER WHEN RUNNING YOUR EXPERIMENT

Remember that the only thing you are changing is whether you are using slime or a glue stick to stick items. All other things should stay the same!

- What items will you try to stick with the glue and slime?
- Will you use slug or snail slime? Or both?

DATA

- How will you test or measure how strong the glue and slime are?

WHAT DID YOU LEARN FROM YOUR EXPERIMENT? WHAT HAPPENED? WHY DO YOU THINK IT HAPPENED?

Real-life application

SLUGS AND SNAILS USE THE SLIME TO STICK TO TRICKY SURFACES. IT ALLOWS THEM TO CLIMB TREES AND PLANTS AND EVEN CRAWL UPSIDE DOWN!

ADVANCED LEVEL: What other questions do you have about slug or snail slime? Design an experiment to answer a question.

EXPLORE: RAISE BUTTERFLIES

Buy a butterfly kit and watch as your caterpillars grow and change into butterflies.

MATERIALS

☐ Butterfly kit

HELPFUL HINTS

- I strongly recommend a kit such as the kind listed in Appendix A that includes host plants rather than a food medium for a more authentic experience.
- Try not to handle your caterpillars.
- See if you can find a way to measure or track your caterpillar's growth.

Extensions

READ BOOKS ABOUT THE BUTTERFLY LIFE CYCLE.

MEASURE AND RECORD YOUR CATERPILLAR'S GROWTH.

READ ABOUT OTHER INSECTS, SUCH AS LADYBUGS, THAT HAVE SIMILAR LIFE CYCLES.

CHALLENGE: DESIGN A MINIATURE AQUARIUM

Here on Earth, water, air, and other nutrients move through a cycle. In a cycle, things like water move from one place to another (for instance, water might move from a lake to a cloud, and then rain down from the cloud to a river), rather than being used up and gone forever. It can be challenging to set up a miniature world where the cycles work well, but when it comes to small freshwater snails and freshwater aquatic plants, it's easy to be successful. In this activity, you'll get to create a sealed aquarium in a bottle. The waste from the snails will provide the nutrients the plants need to grow and the plant (and plants that grow in the water called algae) will provide the food the snails need to grow. It's like creating your own miniature world!

MISSION: Design a miniature aquarium for a freshwater aquatic plant and small aquatic pond snails.

MATERIALS

☐ Plastic container with sealing lid

☐ Aquarium rocks

☐ Aquatic plant

☐ Aquatic pond snails

HELPFUL HINTS

- You will need some sunlight, but keep your container out of direct sunlight or it may get too hot and your plant and snails will die. Placing your aquarium near a window is perfect.

- Pet stores want to get rid of the aquatic pond snails, so you can usually get them for free.

- Please remember that many aquatic plants and aquatic pond snails from the pet store are invasive and cannot be released into the wild.

EXPLORE: TEMPERATURE CHANGES AND INSECTS

Place your insects in various places around your house to see how different temperatures change their behavior.

MATERIALS

☐ One type of insect (for example, crickets, ladybugs, and isopods)

☐ Containers for your insects

DATA

- How will you decide if your insect has changed its behavior?

HELPFUL HINTS

- Allow enough time for your insect to adjust to the new temperature.

- Please do not put your insects in temperatures lower than 33 degrees Fahrenheit or near temperatures higher than 85 degrees Fahrenheit.

- It is fine to place insects in the refrigerator for a brief period of time (20 to 40 minutes will not harm them).

- It is fine to place insects near a heat source (such as a heater vent), but please do not place them in or on a heat source.

Extensions

CAN YOU GUESS WHICH TEMPERATURE YOUR INSECT IS MOST COMFORTABLE IN?

WHAT DO HUMANS DO IN HIGH AND LOW TEMPERATURES? DO YOU THINK INSECTS CAN DO THESE THINGS?

EXPERIMENT: WHAT FOOD DOES YOUR INSECT LIKE?

Can you guess what sort of food your insect will like? Will their favorite food be something from outside? Or will they like something from your kitchen?

MAKE YOUR GUESS: Which of the foods you are trying do you think your insect will like?

THINGS TO CONSIDER WHEN RUNNING YOUR EXPERIMENT

Remember that the only thing you are changing is the type of food. All other things should stay the same!

- Try different foods. Take a look at where your insect lives in nature and be sure to choose some foods from that environment.
- You can offer several different foods at once.

DATA

- How will you decide which food your insect likes best?

WHAT DID YOU LEARN FROM YOUR EXPERIMENT? WHAT HAPPENED? WHY DO YOU THINK IT HAPPENED?

SAMANTHA, AGE 5, PREPARED A TRAY WITH SOME DAMP WOOD, FLOWERS, GRASS, LEAVES, DAMP MOSS, AN APPLE SLICE, AND A STRAWBERRY. SHE ADDED 20 LADYBUGS AND COVERED THE TRAY WITH PLASTIC WRAP WITH SMALL HOLES PUNCHED IN IT. SAMANTHA CHECKED EVERY 10 MINUTES FOR HALF AN HOUR. SHE NOTICED LADYBUGS WERE MOSTLY ON THE APPLE, WOOD, STRAWBERRY, AND MOSS. SHE COULDN'T TELL WHETHER THEY WERE EATING THOSE FOODS OR LICKING THEM TO GET WATER.

ADVANCED LEVEL: What other questions do you have about insects and food? Design an experiment to answer a question.

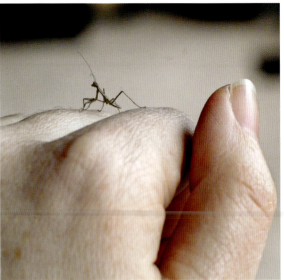

EXPLORE: RAISE PRAYING MANTISES

Order a praying mantis egg case and keep it in a container that has very small air vents. Hatchlings are tiny and can easily escape many cages. A butterfly tent is a great example of an appropriate container. Once your praying mantises hatch, either release them or buy wingless fruit flies from a local pet store to feed them.

MATERIALS:

☐ Praying mantis egg case

☐ A container

☐ Wingless fruit flies (these can be purchased at many pet stores)

HELPFUL HINTS

- Keep a watchful eye to try to catch the egg case hatching. Each egg case contains hundreds of hatchlings. It is quite the sight to see!
- You can (gently) handle the baby mantises, but be warned—they are fast!

Extensions

READ ABOUT PRAYING MANTISES.

OBSERVE THE PRAYING MANTISES EATING WINGLESS FRUIT FLIES.

INVESTIGATE A MOLTED SKELETON. (A MOLT IS WHAT IS LEFT BEHIND WHEN AN INSECT GROWS BIGGER. IT LOOKS LIKE A TRANSPARENT SHELL OF THE INSECT.)

EXPERIMENT: DOES YOUR INSECT PREFER LIGHT OR DARK?

Does your insect prefer being in sunlight or would it rather be underground or in the shade? Or maybe it likes both?

MAKE YOUR GUESS: Do you think your insect prefers light or dark?

THINGS TO CONSIDER WHEN RUNNING YOUR EXPERIMENT

Remember that the only thing you are changing is the amount of light. All other things should stay the same!

- How will you make it light or dark for your insect?
- You can offer a choice between the two at the same time (for example, a box that is half light and half dark).

DATA

- How will you decide if your insect prefers light or dark?

WHAT DID YOU LEARN FROM YOUR EXPERIMENT? WHAT HAPPENED? WHY DO YOU THINK IT HAPPENED?

TIM, AGE 7, CREATED A BOX THAT WAS HALF SHADED AND HALF OPEN TO LIGHT. HE ADDED 10 ISOPODS (PILL BUGS) AND CHECKED EVERY 5 MINUTES FOR 20 MINUTES. TWO BUGS WERE IN THE LIGHT (AND TRIED TO CRAWL OUT OF THE BOX), FIVE CRAWLED UNDER A FLAP IN THE BOTTOM OF THE BOX, AND THREE CRAWLED IN THE FAR SHADED CORNER OF THE BOX.

ADVANCED LEVEL: What other questions do you have about insects and light or dark? Design an experiment to answer a question.

EXPERIMENT: DOES YOUR INSECT PREFER MOIST OR DRY GROUND?

Would your insect rather be moist or dry? Which sort of environment would it rather live in?

MAKE YOUR GUESS: Does your insect prefer moist or dry ground?

THINGS TO CONSIDER WHEN RUNNING YOUR EXPERIMENT

Remember that the only thing you are changing is whether the ground is moist or dry. All other things should stay the same!

- How will you make it moist or dry for your insect?
- You can offer a choice between the two at the same time (for example, a box that is half moist and half dry).

DATA

- How will you decide if your insect prefers moist or dry ground?

WHAT DID YOU LEARN FROM YOUR EXPERIMENT? WHAT HAPPENED? WHY DO YOU THINK IT HAPPENED?

Real-life application

WHERE IS YOUR INSECT FOUND IN NATURE? DOES YOUR EXPERIMENT MATCH WITH HOW YOUR INSECT BEHAVES IN NATURE?

ROSA, AGE 8, DREW A LINE IN A BOX AND GATHERED GRASS FROM OUTSIDE FOR BOTH SIDES. ON ONE SIDE SHE PATTED DOWN THE GRASS WITH A PAPER TOWEL TO MAKE SURE IT WAS NICE AND DRY. SHE SPRAYED THE OTHER SIDE 8 TIMES WITH A SPRAY BOTTLE FULL OF WATER. SHE PLACED 8 ISOPODS (PILL BUGS) IN THE MIDDLE OF THE BOX AND THEN CHECKED WHERE THEY WERE AFTER 10 MINUTES. ALL THE BUGS WENT TO THE BOTTOM OF THE BOX UNDER THE GRASS, SO ROSA HAD TO HUNT FOR THEM. AT THE END OF HER EXPERIMENT, SHE FOUND 5 PILL BUGS ON THE MOIST SIDE OF THE BOX AND 3 ON THE DRY SIDE.

ADVANCED LEVEL: What other questions do you have about moisture and your insect? Design an experiment to answer a question.

EXPERIMENT: DOES YOUR INSECT REACT TO STRONG SMELLS?

Do you think your insect can sense strong smells? Does it seem to like some smells? Are there other smells it avoids?

MAKE YOUR GUESS: Do you think your insect will notice and react to strong smells?

THINGS TO CONSIDER WHEN RUNNING YOUR EXPERIMENT

Remember that the only thing you are changing is adding scents to your insect's environment. All other things should stay the same!

- What scents will you add to your insect's environment? (Hint: a cotton ball works well for liquid scents)
- You can add a few scents at a time.

DATA

- How will you decide if your insect notices or reacts to the scents?

WHAT DID YOU LEARN FROM YOUR EXPERIMENT? WHAT HAPPENED? WHY DO YOU THINK IT HAPPENED?

MACIE, AGE 5, ADDED FOUR POM POMS TO A GLASS DISH. SHE ADDED ABOUT 1 TEASPOON OF VANILLA EXTRACT TO ONE POM POM, 1 TEASPOON OF LEMON EXTRACT TO ANOTHER, 1 TEASPOON OF ORANGE EXTRACT TO ANOTHER, AND 1 TEASPOON OF PEPPERMINT EXTRACT TO THE LAST POM POM. SHE ADDED 8 ISOPODS (PILL BUGS) AND WAITED 20 MINUTES, CHECKING IN EVERY FEW MINUTES. SHE FOUND THAT THE GLASS SURFACE WAS REALLY HARD FOR THE BUGS TO CRAWL ON AND THAT TWO BUGS CRAWLED OVER TO THE VANILLA EXTRACT POM POM AND STAYED THERE FOR 10 MINUTES. THE BUGS IGNORED THE OTHER POM POMS.

ADVANCED LEVEL: What other questions do you have about insects and smells? Design an experiment to answer a question.

Where to Find the Supplies Listed in the Book

The majority of the supplies needed for this book can be purchased at a regular grocery store. However, there is a handful of specialty supplies, many of which are optional, that appear throughout the book. Below is a list of specialty supplies and where we purchased them.

DISCOUNT SCHOOL SUPPLY

- [ ] Stopwatch
- [ ] Tape measure
- [ ] Colored pom poms
- [ ] Colored masking tape
- [ ] Child-safe thermometer
- [ ] Spray bottles

AMAZON

- [ ] Agar powder
- [ ] Petri dishes
- [ ] Plastic beakers
- [ ] Pipettes
- [ ] Plastic binder dividers

- [ ] VOSS water bottle
- [ ] Colored straws
- [ ] Toy frogs
- [ ] Citric acid powder
- [ ] Praying mantis egg case

MICHAELS (OR ANOTHER LOCAL CRAFT STORE)

- [ ] Foam sheets
- [ ] Sticky Velcro
- [ ] Plaster of paris
- [ ] Cardstock paper
- [ ] Hot glue gun
- [ ] Colored wooden craft sticks
- [ ] Pipe cleaners (chenille stems)
- [ ] Wilton candy colors
- [ ] Bud vases

LOWE'S (OR ANOTHER HOME IMPROVEMENT STORE)

- [ ] Children's goggles
- [ ] Plexiglass sheets
- [ ] Potting soil
- [ ] Wood scraps for car ramps

DOLLAR TREE

- [ ] Glass gems
- [ ] Pony beads
- [ ] Lemon juice
- [ ] Rubber bands
- [ ] Markers
- [ ] Baking soda
- [ ] Cotton balls

SHADY OAK BUTTERFLY FARM

- [ ] Butterfly kit with host plants

Resources

FUN AT HOME WITH KIDS ONLINE

You can find even more of our activities at www.funathomewithkids.com.

TEN OTHER INSPIRING SITES

Buggy and Buddy
www.buggyandbuddy.com

Tinkerlab
www.tinkerlab.com

Science Sparks
www.science-sparks.com

Planet Smarty Pants
www.planetsmarty.com

Science Bob
www.sciencebob.com

Left Brain Craft Brain
www.leftbraincraftbrain.com

Lemon Lime Adventures
www.lemonlimeadventures.com

Teach Preschool
www.teachpreschool.org

Kids Play Box
www.kidsplaybox.com

Inspiration Laboratories
www.inspirationlaboratories.com

OTHER INSPIRING BOOKS

150+ Screen-Free Activities for Kids by Asia Citro

Tinkerlab by Rachelle Doorley

Nurturing Inquiry by Charles Pearce

THANK YOU

Thank you to Tiffany Ard of Nerdy Baby for the use of one of her prints:

Nerdy Baby
www.nerdybaby.com
creative@tiffanyard.com

Thank you to Discount School Supply and Shady Oak Butterfly Farm for providing some of the materials we used in this book:

Discount School Supply
1-800-627-2829
www.discountschoolsupply.com

Shady Oak Butterfly Farm
1-877-485-2458
www.butterfliesetc.com
officeteam@shadyoakbutterflyfarm.com

Index

Photo courtesy of Holly Aprecio Photography

About the Author

Asia Citro has an MEd in Science Education and was a classroom science teacher for many years before deciding to stay home full time after the birth of her daughter. She lives near Seattle with her wonderful husband, two awesome children, and two destructive cats. She started her blog *Fun at Home with Kids* in February 2013 and has since spent many late nights experimenting with new play recipes and sensory materials. Her first book, *150+ Screen-Free Activities for Kids*, was published in November 2014. To read about her most recent late-night discoveries or to see more photos of her adorable kids at play, visit www.funathomewithkids.com.